Training Difficult People
Creative tactics for eliminating bad behavior

by Becky Pike Pluth

TRAINING DIFFICULT PEOPLE

Creative tactics for eliminating bad behavior

By Becky Pike Pluth

Dedication

To all the difficult participants I have encountered whose creative challenges have kept me on my feet and continually trying new techniques to move them to learner as quickly and successfully as possible.

Training Difficult People

©2018 Creative Training Productions LLC. All rights reserved.

Text copyright: Becky Pike Pluth

ALL RIGHTS RESERVED

No part of this publication may be reproduced, stored in a retrieval system, or transmitted in any form or by any means, electronic, mechanical, photography, photocopying, recording, scanning, translating into other languages or otherwise without prior written permission from the publisher, except to quote brief passages by a reviewer for critical reviews or articles or as permitted under the United States 1976 Copyright Act.

Trademarks

Many of the designations used by manufacturers and sellers to distinguish their products are claimed as trademarks. Where those designations occur in this book, and Creative Training Productions LLC was aware of a trademark claim, the designations appear as requested by the owner of the trademark. All other product names and services identified throughout this book are used in editorial fashion only and for the benefit of such companies with no intention of infringement of the trademark. No such use, or the use of any trade name, is intended to convey endorsement or other affiliation with this book.

No Liability

The publisher and author hold no liability for any instruction in this book or software/hardware described herein which may cause loss or damage, either directly or indirectly. No warranty may be created or extended.

ISBN: 978-0-9896615-9-1
10 9 8 7 6 5 4 3 2 1
Printed in the United States of America

Credits

Cover Design by Imagewerks
Internal Layout by Alan Pranke
Edited by Liz Wheeler

Publisher

Creative Training Productions LLC
14530 Martin Drive
Eden Prairie MN 55344

For additional books or quantity discounts, contact:

The Bob Pike Group
Phone: 800-383-9210 and 952-829-1954
Fax: 952-829-0260
Email: info@bobpikegroup.com

Table of Contents

Acknowledgements. 9
Dealing with a Difficult Learner. 13
The Blabbermouth 17
The Buzzkill 23
The Class Clown 27
The Defeated 31
The Elder 37
The Fighter. 43
The Hangry 47
The Highjacker. 51
The Hungover 57
The Introvert 61
The Know-It-All. 65
The Latecomer 71
The Petty Rule Breaker. 75
The Preoccupied. 81
The Prisoner. 85
The Sleeper. 91
The Slowpoke. 97
The Texter 103
The Time Thief. 109
The Tweety Bird. 115
The Unprepared. 119
The Unqualified 125
The Vacationer 131
Where to Go *(additional resources)* 135

Acknowledgements

Sometimes I am amazed that another book has been written when I am busy running a business, being a wife (of one) and mom to our four kids, and traveling for my job. This would not be possible if not for my Abba Father who has given me the determination to write amidst what could be seen as chaotic and trying times. God has given me wonderful people who have come alongside to support and encourage me through those life challenges so that I could complete this project. Thank you for being the ultimate giver of grace and a perfect example of managing others' poor behavior! I'm thankful I have such a great role model.

To Tom Richards who is The Bob Pike Group's chief operating officer and one of my longest standing friends. It was you who pushed me to get this project done and was even willing to come alongside and help write the descriptions for each of the "characters." This was just the motivation I needed when I was stuck. What would've taken me five more hours to craft, you crafted in moments. Your gift for writing has been a gift to me and this book. Tom, I'm so glad that you were a youth leader for so many years and had a lot of stories from which to draw. We had a good many laughs determining who the cast of characters would be, and I'm grateful for your help. You were the catalyst in getting this project off the ground, and I'm sure it still wouldn't be written if it wasn't for your pushing me to get er' done.

To Jack and Kate Larsen. A grand majority of this book was written at your cabin up north in Minnesota. The fall is a beautiful time up there with crisp air and loons still hanging out. It was unusually warm while I was writing this book, so I was able to spend time outdoors refreshing my mind, walking with the Lord, and enjoying His nature. Thank you for the gift of a peaceful, quiet and beautiful place to rest and write. Writing goes so fast when your mind can calm down and be creative, and your cabin provided just that.

To my sister Sara. During the writing process, I called you several times, sometimes needing encouragement, and you were there to give it. When I wanted to stop writing and just finish the book "later," it was you that said, "Stay and finish." Thank you for being a rock for me.

To all The Bob Pike Group trainers, present and past. Along the way, many of you have given me ideas to use from your years of practice. Some of these are specifically from your stories, your lives, and our chain of "what would you do" emails!

Doug McCallum, you are one of my biggest champions in training and life. You are also one of the people who has given me advice surrounding difficult behaviors in the classroom from your fifty years of experience. I remember when you once told me that there were only four things one needs to do to overcome any difficult participant. Then, awhile later, I received an email from you about the worst, craziest participant behaviors. From that epic experience, you gave me so many tools to use with my own classes. Thank you for sharing so I could grow and learn and know I wasn't the only one with crazies in my sessions. Thank you!

To my husband and kids. Sometimes I try these tactics on each of you. The ones that didn't work are not in the book! Thank you for loving me and reminding me how important education is and how books help us grow. And no, I don't think I am capable of writing a book on the Reformation!

I'll leave that to the scholars!

To my family. Mom, you always think I'm amazing even when what I've written doesn't make sense. If you had not written my papers in elementary school, this wouldn't be the case! (I so wish that statement was actually true.)

To my three brothers and two sisters who have always been there through each step in my career. Each of you has also role modeled managing difficult behaviors with your own families or on my kids. Thank you.

And Grandma Pat, I wouldn't leave you out. You are a bright light full of wisdom and love and always have time to listen.

Thank you all for helping me forge ahead.

Dealing with a Difficult Learner

Training brings with it a variety of challenges, including difficult behaviors in people we think should want to learn. For goodness sake, they are being paid to be in this class. Isn't that enough motivation?

These challenges often push content to the wayside because so much of the allotted time is spent attempting, sometimes successfully and other times not so much, to get that individual back on track.

It takes just one person to quickly derail the most well-designed training class, workshop, facilitation process, or conference breakout session. A difficult participant is, by definition, someone who disrupts or interferes with the learning of others and himself. This disruption also makes it difficult for that difficult participant to learn.

To combat these bad behaviors and turn the learning tide in your favor, arm yourselves with tactics to help turn around those reluctant or difficult learners.

The first step in dealing with these behaviors is to be prepared. Make sure you have done your homework, have measurable course objectives, know who your audience will be, and have adequately researched and organized your material. Negative behavior types like the know-it-all or blabbermouth are exhibited when the slightest hint of your self-doubt regarding the content is displayed. Be believable, confident, and armed with data or resources to keep learners wanting more.

In the classroom, make sure the lighting is good, that your visual aids or posters are up, and that the music creates a welcoming and positive ambiance as people enter. I also make a point to personally greet participants. This gives me a chance to start putting names to faces and building rapport.

During training, build in a lot of interactive exercises to keep energy up and people engaged. Also, reward the behaviors you want to see. This encourages those who may not be as engaged to step up their game. It sounds simple, but having an unexpected reward like candy to hand out when someone actively answers your questions is an effective way to reinforce class participation. Random and intermittent rewards work best so learners engage but don't expect a reward. It keeps them curious.

Utilizing a variety of group sizes also is a way to mix things up to keep people engaged. Offer opportunities for learners to reflect by themselves, pair up to do a learning exercise, or engage through small groups. Variety not only is the spice of life, it helps you spice up training, too.

Next, identify the behaviors you see most often in your classes by looking in the table of contents of this book.

I have found that, of the twenty-three behaviors covered in this book, the latecomer, the texter, the introvert, the know-it-all, the blabbermouth, the sleeper and the prisoner are the behaviors I most commonly see in my classrooms, and in that order.

Then, if you don't have time to read the entire book all the way through right away, read those chapters representing those most common behaviors. It's like just-in-time training.

You'll notice some of the tips, like having an offline discussion or keeping the difficult participant nearby, work with multiple behavioral issues.

Finally, highlight the strategies that resonate best with you and your style as well as the organization with which you are working. If you are doing a public session with several different companies represented, it may not be possible to have an offline conversation with a manager.

Before dealing with my share of difficult participants, I used to have more experienced trainers on speed dial, which is still not a bad idea if you're feeling unsure. Now, however, you can also use this book and carry it with you for a just-in-time refresher.

There is obviously a lot more you can do to be prepared for a training. For a more in-depth look at how to be prepared and get creative with your training so you can effectively engage all learners, check out *Creative Training: A Train-the-Trainer Field Guide*.

The Blabbermouth

This person can't. Stop. Talking.

If there's a way to say it in ten words, she'll use 100. If it doesn't really matter, he'll talk about it anyway. The blabbermouth doesn't even know it's happening. She loves the sound of her own voice. He's not even listening—he's already preparing his response.

The blabbermouth eats up class time with more questions, interjections, and the last word. The blabbermouth distracts others with too many stories, side conversations, jokes, and commentary. The blabbermouth likes to give advice.

When you see a blabbermouth running your class off the rails, try redirecting tactics like these:

1. **Name tag scramble.**
   Have participants write their names on one name tag and, on a second tag, have them write information others should know about them. For instance, have them list how many years they've been a trainer, one

thing they enjoy doing as a hobby, and one thing that's related to your content like one thing they already know about XYZ. Instruct them to find at least three different people to share with and hear from in the next four minutes. This exercise allows the blabbermouth to get some other words out right away before class begins. Believe me, taking a few minutes to open your session well will give you that much more time before the blabbermouth feels the need to use more words.

2. **Small group discussions.**
This is a relatively easy way for the talkative person to get some other words out at an appropriate time. Be sure to add a few extra small group discussions throughout your day as you notice the blabbermouth beginning to get off-track and disrupting peers at his table. Whenever you begin to notice this happening, strategically place another small-group discussion or have them share with partners.

3. **Provide choices.**
Providing options not only helps a blabbermouth, but it also helps the introvert. Allow participants to choose whether they want to work in pairs or work alone. By giving this option, the introvert, who is exacerbated at this point, can recover while the blabbermouths get together and continue to work things out verbally. It's truly a win–win situation.

4. **Large group share.**
From time to time, consider allowing participants to share their experiences and stories. When you notice the blabbermouth raising his hand, call on someone else first. This way, he will listen to the first person in hopes of getting the next chance. Then ask for one more example and select the blabbermouth if you think he is in need of a talk session. Be clear with time frames when doing this so he doesn't take the class down a rabbit trail.

5. **Rotate the team leader role.**
Each time you have a small group discussion or exercise, select a team

leader. Be sure to watch that leadership is rotating so the talkative participant doesn't always take the stage. For example, you may start off by randomly selecting a leader by birthday closest to today or earliest wake-up time. Later on, as you notice the blabbermouth taking over, use physical attributes to select who will take the lead. As an example, select a leader by shortest hair or person wearing the most bling. This way you know exactly who will be the team leader at the blabbermouth's table. Be specific that the table leader must be the first person to share.

6. **Rotate table groups.**
Because blabbermouths find each other, it is likely they could be at the same table. This makes socializing a little too easy. By switching up table groups, you can split them up and limit their impact.

7. **Use proximity.**
A very quiet way to reengage a talkative person is to do a walking lecturette. Simply share concepts and ideas while you walk around the room. Naturally pause when you get next to the blabbermouth who is carrying on a side conversation. I'm sure you have felt when someone has been in your personal space. Proximity is the quiet invader that helps the wayward talker refocus.

8. **Use chimes.**
Instead of using your voice, try using a chime or something other than your voice to regain the learners' attention after an activity or discussion. Your voice sounds like another voice in the classroom or background noise. You may end up with a dry, sore throat after trying to break through the din several times. My preferred chime is Woodstock's Trio Zenergy chime. It is durable for travel and has a nice distinct tone for each chime.

9. **Use a reward system.**
Reward what you want repeated. If you are having trouble getting a blabbermouth to calm down, give away three points to the first table

seated and ready to learn. Intrinsic and extrinsic reward can be very motivating. Or consider having some of your worksheets be word bank clues and fill-in-the-blanks. This way the individual is racing to complete her sheet and focused on learning versus talking it out. After everyone has completed it, give them a chance to share their answers with the person sitting next to them. So, in this case, the reward for getting the work done is being able to talk!

10. Vocal variety.

A monotone voice makes it easy for learners to lose focus and distract others. Using vocal variety creates energy and enthusiasm and displays passion. Talkers like to listen to talkers who demonstrate excitement and enthusiasm in their voice. Another technique is to quiet your voice down. Most times our instinct is to get louder and just talk over the blabbermouth, but a quiet voice makes the blabbermouth's conversation seem louder and gives his small group the opportunity to shush him.

11. Pause and wait.

Instead of just jumping into your next piece of content after an exercise, discussion, or activity, try pausing until everyone is focused on you. Think about the last time you were in a meeting or at a convention when the keynoter or executive stood up to speak. The room quickly became quiet. This is what you are looking for in your class. Have a smile on your face and a content spirit, and soon the room will be in the palm of your hand. Be careful not to give off a condescending vibe, whether through your facial expressions or in your nonverbal behaviors. This can make the rest of the room uncomfortable when you are just trying to reach one person. Oftentimes raising one hand can also help learners distinguish that you are pausing and waiting.

12. Allow peer pressure.

Why take on the rule of disciplinarian when group members can do it for you? Participants work harder for one another than they do for the speaker. Knowing this, let the group say something to the learner who is speaking out of line. Peers put pressure on the blabbermouth instinctively.

13. Call an audible.

It is one thing when the blabbermouth is talking while the instructor is talking, and it's another when she chooses to do this when her peer is talking. It's your role as the instructor to put this to a stop and quickly. When a peer is sharing and you hear talking coming from a table, give the speaker a "one moment" statement or nonverbal, and just glance in the direction of that table and say, "Thank you for listening to your peer."

14. Ground rules reminder.

Before class starts, create a poster with a few ground rules such as: put phones on silent, connect with people you don't know, or silence is golden when others are talking. If side chatter is becoming a problem, refer back to the ground rules and thank them for being considerate to others.

15. Offline conversation.

Don't belabor the point. Just tell the blabbermouth you are grateful he is in the class because of the wonderful ideas he brings. At the same time, say it would be helpful if he could focus more quickly so the class can keep on pace. Thank him again for being such a great participant, encouraging others to share, and being a valuable part of your class.

16. Public announcement.

When all else fails or you have a class full of blabbermouths, you may need to make a public announcement to emphasize what is in it for them when they refocus quickly—this could be ending on time or leaving a bit early or having a slightly longer break. Let them know the longer it takes for the group to get back on track, the less time there is for content, lunch, and breaks.

The Buzzkill

When a co-worker asked Matt how he liked driving around in a $60,000 loaner vehicle, he said, "Well, for one thing, it gets really bad mileage." The co-worker asked if it was fun being higher up in an SUV. Matt replied, "I always bump my knee getting in." The co-worker said the larger frame must feel safer. Matt said, "Well, it's really hard to park."

What do you call a person who finds the worst in everything? In *The Father of the Bride*, the wedding planner taunts Steve Martin's character, George Banks, by saying, "Every party needs a pooper, that's why we invited you." It seems like every workshop needs a pooper, too, also known as a buzzkill.

There's just no making a buzzkill happy. The room is too cold—wait, now it's too hot. He doesn't want to work with a partner or play any of those silly training games. Nothing is right.

There's no changing a buzzkill in the short time you'll have. But the following tactics work to help them get over the small stuff.

1. **Apply the What's In It For Me principle.**
   At the beginning of class, after you have reviewed the agenda and learners have an idea of the concepts and content that will be shared, allow time for participants to determine what they want to get out of the course. Let them know that it needs to be content related, and finding a significant other shouldn't be the goal! This usually gets a laugh and helps the buzzkill focus on the class at hand. If you hear her saying, "There's nothing here for me," help her brainstorm a couple of different ideas, and ask that she selects one that best meets her needs.

2. **Rotate tables and partners.**
   "People like people like themselves," and in this case, we don't want them at the same table! Consider the last time you had buzzkills in your room. Chances are pretty good they found one another and all became a group! You quickly realize this when you have a team leader sharing back in the large group, and the buzzkill group shares why it won't work for them. The best thing to do is number off your participants and regroup them quickly. If you have twenty-five participants, you would have them number off one through five at each table, and then have a table for each of the numbers. Now you've split them up evenly around the room, and the others at their new table will help squelch the negativity. Do this even if you have just regrouped them into new tables. It will take trouble off your hands.

3. **Utilize small groups.**
   In small groups, there is more accountability and more opportunity for more assertive participants to help you squelch the toxicity that a buzzkill can bring. Frequently, others will share how it could work for them and when your buzzkill says he doesn't like that idea, the other members of the group begin to help provide numerous ways it might work for them. Using small groups takes the full-time job of managing that person off of your shoulders and spreads it amongst a group of people, which is less exhausting for everyone.

4. **Utilize interactivity.**
   Neuroscience shows the brain retains information through

participation and active learning. In order do that, trainers need to give their learners the opportunity to be involved and speak out loud. The brain doing the talking is the one doing the learning. When designing your program, keep in mind that this is a great preventive measure to help with all types of difficult people, especially the buzzkill. Having them up and moving and engaged requires them to play an active role in the process. After they recognize the class is going to be consistently engaging, and there's no way around it, they give up a bit of their whining.

5. **Engage participants with a variety of training methods.**
   What does variety look like? It is more than just lecture and small group discussions. You'll want to think about pair shares, games, clicker-technology use, assessments, job aids, learning partners, physical activities, mental engagers, videos, journaling, action planning, fill-in-the-blanks, or reading relevant text for analysis. These are just a few of the ways to engage participants in a broad manner. If they want to complain about one way, then use a different method. Eventually you'll find at least one activity that works for them. Take note of that and attempt to do another activity that is similar.

6. **Gently correct.**
   Brevity is key. Acknowledge, sympathize or deflect and re-engage buzzkills quickly. Work hard to avoid a verbal battle because the goal is to get the Eeyores engaged in the class and learning something. You could also use a question to engage the individual. Correct them from the standpoint of "I want to help" versus "you need to stop." Remember, you as the instructor need to model excellence both on the stage and off.

7. **Utilize a complaint box.**
   If you are exasperated and don't think you can actually have a conversation with this individual without snapping at her, consider creating a complaint or a "moans and groans" box. Share with the group that you understand this is a difficult process, there's a lot to

be learned, and at times, they may feel the need to vent. Share that everyone in the room deserves an opportunity to focus and be in a positive environment, but at the same time, they may need to get something off their chest. Tell them to feel free to write it down and stick it in the box, so it allows them to get out of a stuck mode and shift gears so they can move forward.

8. **Listen and acknowledge.**

    There are times when a complaint can actually be legitimate. Just because this person has been a naysayer for other reasons doesn't mean there won't be a moment where she really does need a listening ear. At break time, after you have collected yourself and prepared for the next segment, find this individual and open a conversation by asking an open-ended question. This will allow her to share with you her thoughts and opinions to which you can respond, "I'm sorry that is so challenging for you. I will continue to do my best to make this a great experience for you."

    Also consider using short and sweet phrases that give the buzzkill the impression you're listening and validating but not necessarily agreeing. Phrases could be "Wow" or "Interesting" or "I never knew that." Work hard to not roll your eyes, check your phone, or fiddle with anything. Just nod your head and say, "I hear you."

9. **Offline conversation.**

    Be polite, professional, and firm. Whatever you do, don't indicate the buzzkill has gotten under your skin. When break rolls around and other participants vent about the person to you, listen and nod, but keep your opinions to yourself. This is a clear sign that it's time to go further.

    An easy way to start the conversation is to ask a question like "Do you want my opinion?" Creating curiosity generally prompts a conversation. If the participant doesn't want your opinion, share that you need his help and how he could respond to the buzzkill differently to make this training a better learning experience for himself and everyone else. Chronic complainers are very difficult to work with in the classroom because they don't see themselves that way.

The Class Clown

Care to laugh?

Mark Twain said, "Better to remain silent and be thought a fool than to speak and remove all doubt."

Steve Martin said, "Some people have a way with words. And other people, oh, uh, not have way."

Ronald Reagan said, "It has been said that politics is the second oldest profession. I have learned that it bears a striking resemblance to the first."

These are funny lines when delivered to the right people, at the right time, in the right setting. They are clever and smart. They may even make you think.

Humor can be your friend, make your presentation stronger, and win people over quickly. Everyone loves to laugh. And there's nothing like making a room full of other people laugh. Enter the class clown.

The class clown is fueled by attention. She will interrupt or make fun. He will mimic and mock. She will run the clock with stories. He will tease playfully. The class clown goes overboard.

The problem with class clowns is they aren't clever—they're silly. They don't make you think. And they don't make training better—they distract. They're appropriateness' ugly cousin.

Don't let class clowns make your training a punch line. Try this instead.

1. **Humor them...for a time.**
   People who have natural humor can be extremely witty and funny! Laughter in the classroom is a wonderful thing until it takes center stage. Content is king, so it's important we balance the clown's humor with what we need to get done. If it goes on too long or takes up too much time, then you'll need to apply other tactics. Don't go directly to alienating the clown because he can be an asset to your training, especially if you're not witty and humorous. Take a page from his playbook by adding onto his wittiness and tying it back to content.

2. **Laugh with the class.**
   It's okay to find something funny so long as it's appropriate and not offensive. Sometimes there's just the perfect punch line. If it truly is harmless and funny, laugh with the group! It shows that you're human and you know how to have fun and teach at the same time. When the clown starts to mess around with jokes, it's time to wrangle her in and set some boundaries. Until then, enjoy a good laugh.

3. **Learn participants' names.**
   Dale Carnegie said, "A person's name is to that person the sweetest and most important sound in any language." By using first names well in class, we make individuals feel important. It also creates a level of trust and respect faster than calling someone a generic "Hey, you" or pointing at someone and saying, "Go ahead and share." By learning the clown's first name and using it regularly, the need for attention is being met.

4. **Quicken your pace.**
   Make it hard for the clown to get a word in edgewise. By quickening the pace of the course and limiting opportunities to work alone in

silence, there's barely enough time for the show to go on. Don't think of this as a race but rather a brisk walk. Give people breathing time but not so much that they have idle time on their hands or your classmate can turn it into a one-man show.

5. **Use learning partners interactively.**
   There's very little time to get derailed when you keep participants engaged in a variety of activities. Doing partner work allows for that class clown to enjoy meeting new people and gain attention one-on-one while also getting work done. Partner work provides for the largest amount of attention, so consider using more of these types of activities during your course.

6. **Rotate tables so the clown gets around.**
   Be watchful for how long the group can take a certain individual. When an adult is acting like a teenager, it can get daunting for others. Mix it up every three hours for best results. If you have a substantially wackier learner, you may want to mix it up even more, but not more than three times a day or the rest of the class will get annoyed with having to move yet again. As they find a new group, be sure to ask the class to brainstorm reasons why switching tables is a good thing.

7. **Use proximity and perhaps a slight touch on the shoulder.**
   If the obnoxious clown can't stop fooling around, try walking closer to her until you get into her comfort zone. She'll feel your presence while you continue to talk, and it will usually quiet her. If she continues to joke around while you're standing right next to her, consider using a slight tap on the shoulder to quietly shush her. Know your audience and whether or not this person could handle a little tap. I have found that clowns typically like the attention and also get the point that they need to stop.

8. **Dole out positive attention.**
   When the class clown is on task and doing a great job, be sure to walk by and tell him so. Typically, the immature adult is desiring attention

for one reason or another, and this fills his bucket, so he doesn't feel the need to get attention from others in inappropriate ways.

9. **Use silence.**
Wait to move on until everyone's attention is with you. Show that you are gracious yet firm and control the front of the room. Participants are truly in control of the class, but by waiting patiently in silence, you garner a level of respect. Other learners around the clown will also appreciate this because then they can actually hear what you have to say and not have to attempt to listen over the immaturity.

10. **Administer the silent stare.**
Sometimes it just takes a stare with a slight grin to get your silly one back on track. It lets her know that you're going to wait, but it also directs the remainder of the class her way, giving her attention, which we know she loves. Work hard to make that stare work for you instead of it creating an awkward situation.

11. **Immediately stop offensive humor.**
Rarely with the class clown has it ever gotten to the point where I had to stop in the middle of class and ask him to immediately discontinue his behavior. However, when someone has been offensive in front of the group, the group needs to know that something is being done and that you're not standing idly by.

12. **Offline conversation.**
There may be a point when you need to ask the participant to have a private conversation. During a conversation, it's important to have an action plan together. Ask the participant to tell you what he could do differently to make this a better experience for everyone. When the clown comes up with the ideas, he is far more likely to be able to follow through on the commitment. Ask him how you can be of assistance and what would be a good way to remind him silently so he can reengage appropriately. Perhaps a slight nod in his direction is a way to do this.

The Defeated

A little boy was walking with his parents on the beach when he stopped to pick up seashells. When he looked up, he saw his parents a few steps ahead and hurried to catch up. He stopped again to pick up shells. When he looked up, his parents were even further ahead, so he ran to catch up. The third time he stopped to pick up shells, he looked up and his parents were so far ahead, he simply sat down. He didn't even try. He was defeated.

The same thing happens in the workplace when people feel the challenge before them is insurmountable. It happens in training when they feel overwhelmed. When you sense someone is about to throw in the towel, breathe new life into your training following these simple techniques.

1. **Use silent activities.**
    Think about the last time you felt defeated. The first thing you wanted to do was be alone. Silent activities can allow the defeated to regroup, pick himself up again, and save face. It also can provide an opportunity for you to walk over and give a little one-on-one help if needed.

2. **Provide coaching or extra instruction.**
   Providing a little extra time to these individuals goes a long way. It shows you care and want them to be successful. This is easy to do during silent activities but harder during group exercises. During a group activity, walk over to the group during the exercise, and stand right next to the individual. Ask how things are going. Conversation can provide a little extra encouragement she might need. Let her know you are available during part of your breaks to help out or are willing to stay after class to answer any questions. Typically, the defeated will look you up on your break time or after class. (I find it rare for the defeated to come in during lunch.)

3. **Use a handout.**
   Are you a great notetaker? Do you know exactly what the focus points are when someone is speaking? If you answered yes, remember that doesn't come naturally to everyone. By having a handout that includes blank note pages as well as pages with content already structured, you can create a less daunting class for your learners. Chunk the handout into Need To Know, Nice To Know (additional content that could be covered if time allows), and Where To Go (references and additional resources). Be sure to let the group know that it is chunked that way and that you'll be primarily covering the need-to-know section. Knowing that the class won't cover everything in the workbook gives the overwhelmed a better perspective.

4. **Move tables.**
   In this case, it's important for the individual to be at a quieter part of the room. It's much like helping an attention-deficit student focus. Attempt to keep the defeated toward the front because there are fewer distractions and better visibility for visuals there.

5. **Chunk content and instructions.**
   As a trainer, you might lose someone when you show him how to get from A to Z all at one time. But if you can help him figure out how to get from A to B, then from B to C, then from C to D and so on, you'll be a hero.

Micro-learning is chunking content into bite-size pieces that are five minutes or less. When you have a learner who is overwhelmed and feeling defeated, bite-size pieces make things manageable. Consider taking a twenty-minute chunk of content and breaking it into sub topics at five minutes apiece. Then you'll be able to check in with that person on a more frequent basis.

Remember that giving directions can be mind boggling. Just like Map in Dora, provide three directions or less at a time. If there are more than three directions, either chunk them or put them on a PowerPoint slide. For example, you might say, "In just a moment, when I say 'go,' please take a marker and head to the wall with your group. One person will need to get a piece of flip chart paper to place on the wall near your group." Once the groups have all done those three instructions, you can then move onto the next three.

6. **Partner work.**
Using learning partners allows one person to get to know this individual and be able to help her through the course. It builds stability and consistency so that a firm foundation can be laid. Once it is laid, the defeated will feel more comfortable sharing her struggles and asking for help. Keep the same learning partner throughout the course if it's just two or three days. If the course is a six-week course, others can be of assistance.

7. **Apply spaced-learning principles.**
Motivation and application help your learners better remember what they have learned. Spacing, or reviewing information at spaced intervals, is another way to improve content retention. What should spacing look like in our training sessions? Create learning that is scheduled with time in-between. For example, instead of one six-hour class day, it would be better to allow sleep in-between the modules. Teaching three hours one week and then three hours a week later is better. This is especially true for complex content.

Memories grow over time; therefore, time needs to go by in order for new neurons, the brain cells that carry information, to be made. Multiple studies show that cramming is actually associated with low achievement (Hartwig and Dunlosky 2012). For a more in-depth look at spacing, read chapter four of *Creative Training, a Train-the-Trainer Field Guide*.

8. **Use examples, analogies and stories.**
   When the learner is stumped, understanding complex information is possible; the learner just needs to hear the information in a different way. When you see faces that are questioning and look stumped, the first strategy to try is to have small groups come up with their own example, analogy, or story to connect the dots. We want them to do as much of the learning as possible. Making sense and meaning of it in their own words creates better recall and a deeper understanding. Have a team leader share back with the group their example, analogy, or story. This is a way for you to double-check that they are getting the concept. If they're getting it, go ahead and move on. If not, you may need to share your own example or analogy.

9. **Assign specific tasks.**
   The defeated does better with assigned, specific tasks. So, instead of being broad and allowing students to get creative with their outcomes or assignments, give clear instructions, perhaps written instructions coupled with auditory instructions. A very clear focus and objective for the activity simplifies processes for the overwhelmed.

10. **Offer online training resources.**
    If you teach a class that is repeated multiple times, consider creating off-line materials for after class. Micro-learning would be the best solution here because it is presented in less-than-five-minute snippets. When you see one group struggling with concepts, create a couple of micro-learning modules for the next class.

If you're teaching a class one time, ask your peers to review your materials and share with you what they think the hardest topics will be. Then create a couple of micro-learnings as pre-work or homework that can be used for your course. This allows the struggling learner to be able to take her time and reinforce information that was shared during class.

11. **Repeat key ideas.**

    When repeating key ideas throughout the day, don't say or do the exact same thing you said or did before. Rather create an opportunity to study the information in a different way. If in the morning you did a lecture, then play a review game in the afternoon. If earlier in the day you had learners working in partnerships, try a large group discussion in the afternoon. Build time into your course for these revisits should they be needed. If they are not needed, then refer to your Nice-To-Know section and cover a little more content.

The Elder

Elder Ellen likes her flip phone and cassettes. Ellen also hates video conferencing and saving her work to the cloud. Change takes energy and feels daunting. The old ways work fine.

How do you get buy-in from your group of elders? So many times, these are the people with the most institutional knowledge, and it's critical that knowledge is recognized, tapped, and transferred as much as possible.

Like a pendulum, the people who bring the most experience can also be the most resistant to change. When you see that happening, keep the following tips in mind.

1. **Increase the PowerPoint font size.**
   When teaching in the classroom the usual rules of thumb for slides are a font size of 28 points to 32 points, and no more than six words per line and six lines per slide. However, the problem with these guidelines is a lack of consideration for those in the room who may wear glasses and have forgotten them or whose eyesight is fading a bit. In order to ensure the back rows can see, increase your font size to a minimum of

36 points, or even better, a 42-point font. Also, consider making the text bold and the images larger, and have a strong contrast between the background of the slide and the text.

2. **Move the elders to front tables.**
When rearranging groups, attempt to get the elders to the front of the room, so they can hear better and be more easily engaged because you're right there, too. For the most part, the elder is a good listener but at times may fall asleep. By keeping them close to you, you're able to keep an eye on this and encourage their tables.

3. **Allow more time for learning activities.**
Our seasoned warriors are willing to participate with fervor. To continue that excitement, give them enough time to complete things whether on their own, with a partner, or in a small group. If the conversation is just meant to be started and not completed, let the group know you'll be cutting them off after two minutes. This way they know the expectations and don't feel poorly when an activity or conversation is not completed.

4. **Tap into their life experience.**
This is one of their biggest assets, and it should be used while in class. Acknowledge their vast experience as they enter the room, and ask if they would be willing to share some of their life experience with the rest of the group from time to time. Asking offline and not in front of the rest of the room gives them a chance to consider the request and say yes. This shows them respect and high regard for what they know. Encourage them to share readily with their teams and partners.

5. **Honor experience.**
There are several different ways to honor one's experience. Try having all participants put the number of their years of experience on their name tags, then have small groups add up the number of years and write it on a sticky note. Each group then brings that up and posts it to the front flip chart. Share with the group the number of years

you have. Then share the number of years' experience represented in the room and explain that you'll be learning from one another, the content and you, the trainer.

Another idea is to connect with them on breaks. Find out what they know, what they're excited about, what examples they have that relate. Listen to their work stories that align with what you're teaching. Then ask if they would be willing to share that with the rest of the group. Be sure to let them know you would really appreciate it. Again, let them know it's helpful in making strong connections to the concepts. This gives them the why behind sharing.

6. **Ask-it basket.**
Someone on the older end of the spectrum in your class may have a lot of experience in life but may not have as much experience in the area that you are teaching. In order to help all learners, have an ask-it basket where questions can be placed. Make a commitment to the group that any questions there will either be answered or discussed as a group, or a resource will be provided such as a link, website, journal article or a reference. Those in the room who are a bit nervous about learning something new will rest easier knowing they have a way to get their questions answered without drawing attention to themselves. Answer questions along the way versus waiting till the very end of the day or the class.

7. **Correct in private.**
Any correction, whether with an elder or not, should be done in private. If there's a time where they have misunderstood or are not doing the correct thing, have a conversation off to the side where others won't overhear what you're talking about. The elder will silently be thanking you.

8. **Give praise, encouragement and approval offline.**
This may sound crazy but, unlike other generations, the oldest generation in our workforce does appreciate your praise and approval but may be embarrassed to hear it out loud. It doesn't have to be a

spoken word. They really appreciate a little note or letter. By doing this, you know exactly how much time you will allot, and it connects with them on a deeper level, bringing back memories of letters they once wrote themselves.

9. **Distribute the wealth.**
It is not as valuable to have all of your elders at one table. Although they may connect quickly, it's important to have a variety of ages and experience at tables for cross-sharing. And when technology is being used, it gives a chance for the younger crowd to be helpful as well. Equally distribute the amount of time each individual in the class has to speak. You don't want to alienate anyone but that could be done if you spend too much time with the more mature.

This also applies to how many questions you answer. If you are continually getting questions from the same individual, consider asking groups to discuss an answer and share back or provide a moment for someone at their table to clarify. Doing this allows another learner the opportunity to repeat back his or her learnings while helping a colleague.

10. **Smile often.**
A soft smile and a kind word goes a long way. Nodding your head and giving positive nonverbal cues encourages the more mature. Confidence is an important part of class for these individuals and a simple smile can help boost that.

11. **Avoid patronizing.**
Consider the last time you felt patronized. Being talked down to doesn't feel good. If the goal is to champion learners in your room, think before you speak. Wearing an authentic smile makes it more difficult to have a patronizing tone in your voice, that sing-songy and kindly sarcastic nuance that goes along with treating someone as an inferior.

12. Consider the technology gap.

A majority of our learners are digital natives, meaning they have had computer technologies for a majority of their lives. However, technology for some can cause stress and anxiety. In order to bridge the gap when technologies are being used, pair less experienced tech users with patient digital natives. Be watchful to find who that patient person would be. Another way to bridge the gap is to have a non-tech way to do the high-tech components. For instance, if you are using clicker technology to answer questions on the screen, allow that person to write his or her answer on a whiteboard. To avoid alienating that one person, give the entire class the option. You'll be surprised at how many millennials choose whiteboards and markers just because it's different from what they do all day!

13. Paired shares.

Increase the number of pair shares where people are working one-on-one versus small groups or in a large group. This allows for the elder to feel really confident and a bit confidential as they are sharing one-on-one.

The Fighter

Teenagers are notoriously skeptical of authority. They argue, challenge, and test boundaries. Mark Twain once said, "When I was a boy of fourteen, my father was so ignorant I could hardly stand to have the old man around. But when I got to be twenty-one, I was astonished at how much the old man had learned in seven years." Some adult learners aren't so different.

As a trainer, you're most likely to face fighters who demand to see the research, who question your working assumptions, or who have "tried it before" and believe it won't work. But if you fight back, nobody wins.

Instead of fighting, deescalate the situation by following these ideas:

1. **Use pre-work and questions to consider.**
   When someone jumps out at you from behind the door, you might jump back or let out a little scream. The same is true for our fighter. He gets on the defensive when surprised. By being proactive and having pre-work, you provide an understanding of what's to come. Using a thoughtful question such as asking what learners want to get out of the course before the class has even begun sets a positive tone.

If the fighters choose not to do the pre-work or answer the question, at least they knew it came, and they made a choice versus coming to class and being surprised.

2. **Send a letter that includes an agenda, goals, expectations.**
Like the pre-work and the question to consider, provide an email or welcome letter that covers the details of what's to come. Be clear on the location, the start time, what to wear (such as a light jacket to help adapt to the temperature in the room), or any other expectations you may have of the course.

3. **Be introduced by a respected authority.**
Stanford's Jeffrey Pfeffer did a study which found that having someone else toot your horn can be extremely effective for helping people buy-in compared to introducing yourself and singing your own praises. Other studies have shown the same thing. Whenever possible, ask your manager or perhaps a vice president, or other VIP, to introduce the course and sing your praises, even if you write it up yourself. The fighter, the know-it-all, and the prisoner will all appreciate this and be sold on the training a bit quicker because of it.

4. **Practice the art of persuasion.**
Think about the last purchase you made where you didn't have full confidence in what the sales person was sharing, but you put your faith in who was saying it. It isn't necessarily the message carrying the weight but the messenger. It's your job to persuade the fighter that you have the expertise. Allow her to see your competence without bragging or listing your triumphs. It is okay in class to use examples of situations you were in previously to support content in a common-sense way without bragging. You can always use the word "we" to make it less about you and more about the team.

Another way to be persuasive is to respond logically to emotional statements. Listen and narrate back to the individual in your own words. Let him know that he's been heard and that you would like to ease his concerns. Also consider using starter phrases from your

Communications 101 class that never go out of style, phrases like:
- a. "So what you are saying/asking is…"
- b. "What is important to you is…"
- c. "You'd like to know more about…"
- d. "The central idea of your question/comment is…"

5. **Include a reference section in the handout.**
   Because the fighter is a skeptic, it's best to be prepared. Any research, data, or statistic that you reference should have a source listing to go with it in the where-to-go section or other handout. This way, if you cite research but can't quite remember where it came from, you can refer them to those pages to see for themselves. After citing your sources the first couple of hours, the fighter typically lays off and can readily see the content is researched.

6. **Refer to studies and journal articles.**
   Casually referring to stories in journal articles not only shows your prowess but also builds confidence in your skeptical fighter. Try memorizing at least a couple of your references as well as some of your statistics. If you have a hard time recalling this information, you can pencil it in on your flip chart paper or poster ahead of time, then re-write over it in dark marker as you read the statistic from your poster. This technique comes in handy on those days where your mind just isn't as sharp. If the content isn't well-researched, come up with a couple of journal articles on your own that support the data you are sharing so you have that in your back pocket. As a trainer, this will give you more confidence and makes it more difficult for the fighter to walk all over you.

7. **Use fact-based, practical content.**
   Typically, doubters begin to argue over opinions. Attempt to stay with facts because those are more difficult to argue with, especially if they're well researched. If some of the content is opinion-based, find out why your organization holds the policy it does so that you can at least defend the opinion with facts. If your disbeliever can find value and

utilize the content that you're teaching right away, she is more likely to drop her guard and be a great participant. It may only take fifteen to thirty minutes to win over your disbeliever, so make sure you have that first half hour down pat.

8. **Change table groups.**
   The fighter can be a difficult person to be around for a long period of time. If this individual persists in his evidence-finding and pushing back, be sure to change table groups from time to time to give others a break. A new group may also push back harder on their colleague than the original group. Test the waters until you find a really good group to set this person with and then keep him there. Don't feel the need to change groups just because it's what you always do. If this questioner is doing well, leave him be.

9. **Diffuse negative behavior.**
   If the fighter is publicly negative, this needs to be dealt with publicly. Always use a content and kind spirit when addressing anyone in class but especially with your fighter. At times, it can seem her goal is to start a fight and defeat you. Be ready with a couple of analogies to help change the fighter's perception. For example, when someone says, "The scope of the project is too large to complete with the amount of time and resources we have," come back with an analogy they can easily understand. For instance, you can compare this project to moving from the minor leagues in baseball to the majors. Focus the conversation on the difference between the two leagues, like rules, more difficult opponents, owners with a high level of expectation, etc.

10. **Follow up with participants.**
    Whether using email, a letter or a video, a workshop follow-up through micro-learning gives you the opportunity to summarize key takeaways and present your point of view again. There's nothing like having the last word!

The Hangry

Winnie the Pooh had a rumbly in his tumbly. That's a nice way to say it.

Even the nicest people will turn on you when you run late and cut into their lunch hour or forget to break for morning coffee or afternoon snacks. As blood sugar levels drop and hunger pangs kick in, people get irritable. They get short-tempered. They lose concentration. They are hangry.

The longer the course, or the earlier it starts, or the later it runs, the more this issue comes into play. And the biggest problem is when people are thinking about their tummies, they are not fully engaged with you.

Keep these aces in your back pocket to appease the hangry and keep the focus on learning.

1. **Provide simple snacks.**
   Oftentimes someone other than the trainer is organizing snacks, and it's important to communicate with that person to make sure you have the right combination of items. It doesn't need to be fancy, but it does need to effectively and quickly stop a hangry outbreak. Ask for a combination of protein, whole grains and produce. The produce or

whole grains allows for a quick pick-me-up with carbs and sugars while the proteins have a longer-lasting impact and slower absorption rate into the blood stream, allowing for a longer-term alertness. Consider asking for mangoes and pistachios or apples with raw almonds. Another could be bananas and walnuts or cherry tomatoes and cheese slices. As a backup, purchase a bag of walnuts or raw almonds to offer to a learner in need. This may come out of pocket, but it's an invaluable resource that will make class easier for you.

2. **Provide lunch that helps learning.**
    You may not have control over what is ordered for lunch but connect with the person who does and kindly ask for one of the following examples. This will help not only the low blood sugar person but the whole class. When heavy meals are served, our bodies and brains do heavy lifting to break down that meal. This decreases each body's ability to focus and makes learners sleepy. Think of how you feel after Thanksgiving or a holiday meal after you've eaten too many starches or carbohydrates. The following are a few examples of what could be good for a meal request. If nothing else, consider having it for yourself so that you are at the top of your game.
    a. Breakfast: Oatmeal with blueberries and chia or other types of seeds; even easier is a breakfast bar and a banana
    b. Lunch: Turkey sandwich on nine-grain or whole grain bread with carrot sticks; chicken wrapped with a whole grain tortilla with broccoli and red peppers; vegetable salad with tuna and whole grain rolls
    c. Snacks: Hardboiled egg with whole wheat crackers and an apple; cheese stick, grapes, whole grain crackers
    d. Dinner: Brown rice, chicken breast, asparagus spears; couscous with unsalted cashews, lean beef tips, green beans

    If you're like me after reading that list, it's time for lunch!

3. **Be calm.**
    When this individual gets riled up, it's a good time to pull out the snacks. If you don't have any, remember that calm begets calm. When

the hangry responds in an edgy tone, you are the one who needs to demonstrate what good looks like. To stay calm, try breathing in through your nose and out through your mouth, or have the group stand and do a stretch break which provides you a moment to gather yourself. If possible, have the group take a break which will allow that participant to get something to eat.

4. **Reduce the noise level.**
   Instead of doing activities with partners, try small groups or even a large-group exercise. The greater the number of speakers, the greater the noise in the room. When someone is agitated or edgy, loud noises can exacerbate the problem. Another idea is to play calming music in the background at low levels. This encourages participants to work alone in silence versus feeling free to connect with others while they work. I would also be clear and state that this activity is to be done alone in silence and that learners will have a chance to connect with one another after the brainstorming time.

5. **Turn off music.**
   Typically during activities like relay races, breaks, or lunch, background music can make a stale classroom come to life. When noticing that you have "hungry and angry" personalities in the room, skip the music until they have had a chance to fill their bellies and recover.

6. **Listen and empathize.**
   Sometimes all that is needed is a listening ear. A simple model to show that you are listening is SLANT. Sit up, lean forward, ask questions and repeat back, nod your head, and thank the person for sharing. When you're asking questions and repeating back, that is a good time to use a statement like "I would be asking the same question," or "That would frustrate me, too."

7. **Add a quick snack break.**
   Sometimes it's not time for a break, but we need to add one in quickly. As a trainer, you're also responsible for reading the classroom vibes.

Even if you're only a half-hour into the session but you feel there is no way an individual will make it through the next sixty minutes before break, let the group know you're going to take a quick five-minute, one-and-done break, meaning they have time to complete one activity such as get a drink of water or go to the bathroom or check messages. Then ask the particular individual if he had a chance to eat breakfast or if he would like some nuts. The break provides the opportunity to give this learner a chance to be focused for the next hour.

8. **Include physical interactive activities.**
Think back to when you were working on a really big project like painting a room or completing homework. It's amazing how long people can go without a food break when their bodies are busy. Movement can help take the mind off of the hunger. Have in your toolkit of exercises a couple of general activities that are physical in nature. If you can't recall one, simply take the group on a field trip to another part of the room or outside to teach the next segment. Quick energizers that are physical can work as well. Perhaps a stand-and-stretch, touch three walls, find a partner and share one idea you've learned, or even a dance-off!

9. **Partner work.**
Partner work may increase the noise in the room, but allowing partners to move to a quieter space can bring anxiety down. Allow this learner and her partner to work outside the classroom in the hallway or find a quieter space in the classroom.

10. **Problem solve with the learner.**
When putting the rest of the group into an activity, take time to pull this individual aside and quickly problem-solve to find a solution to his attitude and behaviors. Sometimes the hangry don't even know their behavior is different from others and may not even know that it's because they're hungry. Although you are guessing the root cause is hunger, this can be confirmed and solved with a quick conversation.

The Highjacker

The staff appreciation dinner was going so nicely. It was a catered event at an intimate venue. The night was all about recognizing people's contributions, expressing thanks, and encouraging one another. Until Rick spoke up.

Rick came to dinner with an agenda. He highjacked the event and held it hostage for a few minutes while he listed his grievances and demands. His domineering way made some people uncomfortable and tainted the mood.

"Ricks" are everywhere. They usually mean well. They highjack training sessions by talking too much, barking orders, questioning the instructor, or using their influence to sway the group toward their way of thinking.

Some participants defer to the highjacker while others resent him. But with a few specialized tools in your toolkit, you'll be ready to level off even the biggest personalities to create a safe learning environment for everyone.

1. **Establish ground rules.**
   Assuming that you're going to have at least one difficult participant in the room, write your rules on a poster page and tape it to the floor, so

as participants enter, they read your creatively placed "ground rules." Simple things can be on the list in addition to the one you really want to make sure is on there. Rules can be things like: meet someone new, sign in, grab coffee or a bite to eat. Somewhere within your list add "Avoid hijacking the class or class time." If anyone attempts to do so in the future, you can simply ask them to refer back to the rules that are on the ground by the door. This will save you time and perhaps even a confrontation.

2. **Treat him fairly.**
The hijacker gets treated fairly, not necessarily equally. Some easy ways to be fair include no more and no less time to connect, speak up, be the team leader, or rule the roost as anyone else in the classroom. However, to be fair, reward those in the classroom who are behaving the way you expect. Rewards could be a small piece of candy or a simple sticker they're collecting as an opportunity to win a prize at the end of the class.

3. **Use level-setting exercises.**
Level-setting exercises help a group to be on the same playing level. No one in the room, no matter their years of experience or ability level, has more say because of volume, tenure or title. Examples of level-setting exercises include: a name tag scramble where individuals choose what they want to put on their name tag to share, team leaders who are randomly selected by obscure data points like highest miles on their car, random group work, random partners, or team charts where a group of people find what they have in common or create a chart at the wall and make it relevant to the content being taught for the week. Each of these allows for every individual to have choice and a say which creates a room of equals versus focusing on the more tenured or loudest, AKA "the hijacker."

4. **Establish group questioning.**
When a hijacker is objecting or belittling content, put it back to small groups. Have each table decide what their thoughts are on the content

of his rant. Having peers at his table disagree with him is a great way to squelch the rant. Have table leaders share back their thoughts, and the participants have now solved the problem instead of you. Continue to use this method every single time the Ricks decide to take the stage. Pretty soon his peers are going to tell him to stop. Having the group tell him to stop is a way for you to maintain your stance and keep respect versus having the individual upset with you. Oftentimes the hijacker cares more about what his peers think than what the instructor thinks.

5. **Pause.**
Whenever the domineering individual is using side chatter or disrupting his group, take a moment and pause the lecture and just wait for his voice to be the loudest in the room and for him to recognize he needs to stop. It's not fair to his colleagues who are subjected to him to not have the opportunity to hear what you are sharing. Be careful not to have facial expressions or nonverbals that relay you're ticked off. Instead, a small smile and a glance in his direction is all that's needed. When the individual stops talking, you can either move on or say a quick "thank you" to honor that he's done what you've silently asked.

6. **Move him up front to your non-dominant side.**
Learning this early and using this often can help you with a myriad of difficult participants. You naturally look to engage with the tables that are on your dominant side. By placing Rick up front on your non-dominant side, you're not subjected to looking at him as often, but he is close enough to realize you are right there. The overbearing individual is already getting enough of your attention in other ways so set yourself up for success by planting Rick where he won't get more than necessary.

7. **Involve him.**
You've tried a lot of other tactics, and now it's time to ratchet it up a level. Let Rick be your scribe. He doesn't seem to need to take notes anyway. Be sure you ask him to be a scribe to make it about him. For instance, you could say, "It appears you have a lot of experience with

this content. Would you be willing to be a scribe for me?" Notice you say "it appears." This is because you and I both know the Ricks don't know it all, but they think they have better ideas. By putting them up front with you, it forces them to focus and be less distracting to their group.

8. **Minimize his impact.**
   As quickly as possible, minimize the impact Rick is having on others. When you notice that he is being high-handed, step in. Our job is to get Rick back on track as quickly as possible. It may mean you need to go straight into a partner share or do a quick energizer. Don't always go straight to the disciplinarian-in-action routine; rather, pursue quiet ways to reengage him. There are others in your class, and you want it to be a good experience for all.

9. **Keep your distance.**
   Because the highjacker desires your attention, work with other groups and keep your distance. His goal is to derail the class, and it may seem he is willing to do anything to accomplish that. Putting space between you and him silently says you're not paying attention to him, and subconsciously, he stops until you get closer and can hear what he is saying.

10. **Use humor.**
    If you feel tension in the room, it's time for some humor. Use natural humor about course content or the way things are done versus using jokes that could offend someone. You may want to have a couple of ideas in your back pocket such as a way to pick a team leader that makes everyone laugh. One way to do this is to have everyone put up one pointer finger. When you count to three, have them point at the person at the table who they think should be the next team leader. Then count to three, everyone points, and the class erupts in laughter.

11. **Take criticism with a smile.**
    It is challenging to accept criticism, especially when it's not true. However, remember what Rick is saying is not really about you, it's

about riling you up. When people say things that are caustic or rude, it's saying something about them, not you. Instead, smile and thank Rick for sharing. You're not agreeing that it's true; you're simply ending the conversation. Obviously, if you're teaching children or students, this one should not apply!

12. Avoid reacting.

Being provoked can be really annoying and aggravating. It also can be difficult not to have some sort of reaction. You may even need to turn around and roll your eyes or let out a slight sigh just to keep your cool. It is still your job to keep the content moving. Reacting takes time away from what's important.

13. Limit interactions.

At this point, you're probably exasperated. So it's a good time to stop interacting with this individual. By not interacting, you're limiting the number of offensive things he can say to you and how much he actually aggravates you. Do this by sharing your attention with the other students. When busy with others, he can't take your attention. When groups are working, connect with other groups. Be sure to keep an ear toward his group to be sure he's not getting under anyone else's skin. When you listen but are facing toward another group, you will usually find he is behaving.

14. Use empathy.

This may be simply saying "I can see how it may appear that way..." when Rick has yet another objection. Again, this statement is not agreeing or disagreeing with them, it is just showing empathy.

15. Refuse to argue.

It is important to maintain composure. Because the highjacker's goal is to irritate and try your patience, when you choose not to argue, you win. When you do not engage in this behavior, it shuts Rick down.

16. **Model a positive tone.**

    When others in the class may be frustrated, you need to maintain a positive tone. If you can see others are aggravated, it's time to move to step eighteen or nineteen. If it's not quite there yet, just keep on with your presentation in a joy-filled manner. Don't let Rick steal your passion. Although he may have lit a fire, turn it into passion.

17. **Share boundaries with the group.**

    If you've gotten to this point, you have tried and tried and tried again. Now it's time to set some boundaries. You might tell the group that in order to move forward and create a safe space, some boundaries need to be set. Some of those boundaries could be: keep negative thoughts to yourself, offer solutions versus problems, share when it is helpful to your group, merely say thank you when someone shares instead of sharing your opinion, or lift others up.

18. **Discuss the situation offline.**

    Unfortunately, you may have to have one or more of these offline conversations before, during, and after the course day. Some people just won't give up. They may combine the hijacker with the know-it-all and the fighter. When a learner is demonstrating more than one difficult behavior, invite him to leave the class. It is unlikely he actually will because he enjoys ruffling your feathers. In these off-line conversations, ask him how you can be of help or what it is that is causing his struggles. Try to offer solutions or, even better, ask him what his solution would be. Let him know if he has issues with the class, he should take it up with you later and not during class time.

19. **Invite him to leave; offer a refund.**

    At this point, just pray the highjacker actually takes your offer. He has increased the stress level for you and those around him enough. Amazingly enough, if you've utilized the tactics above, it's very likely the other participants are enjoying the class in spite of the hijacker.

The Hungover

Too much of a good thing is, well, not a good thing.

From time to time, you will find participants in your class who enjoyed too much of a good thing the night before your training. They stayed out too late, drank too much, partied too hard and now look half-dead as you're set to begin a session that needs their focus and buy-in.

The common symptoms of a hangover—headache, fatigue, nausea, decreased motor skills, sensitivity to light or music—can be tough to shake. It's critical to recognize when people aren't quite ready to learn.

Before you begin a session with someone who is hungover, know what company policy is to ensure you keep your job. If policy is to just deal with it, here are some tactics to help you make slight modifications to your class that will make a world of difference when you spot a character like "Doug" and help limit his liability in the classroom.

1. **Change tables.**
   Because Doug is sluggish and perhaps not feeling so well, it's important to get him up and moving. Get that blood flowing. It also takes the pressure off those around him who are noticing the aftereffects of a "fun" night. Switching tables gives Doug's peers a break.

2. **Use physical interactivities.**
   It's time to move into the interactive activity segment of your presentation. If you've planned an hour-long lecture, that's going to be pretty difficult with Doug in the class, but not impossible. Here are some simple ways to get people moving that can be implemented quickly:
   - Take a discussion that was supposed to be done at the table and have people stand to discuss.
   - Have participants find a partner on the other side of the room and do an activity in the workbook.
   - Place answers to blanks in the workbook on the floor; have people stand and fill in the blanks versus sit and fill in the blanks.
   - Have groups get flipchart paper and markers and head to the wall to brainstorm a list of ideas.

3. **Increase energizers throughout the session.**
   Energizers don't necessarily need to be related to the content in order to get the blood flowing. Simple ideas include: stand when you finish filling out the page, or stand when you are done discussing then I'll know you're ready to move on. There are a lot of other energizers that can be done. If you need help finding some quickly, invest in the book *CORE for Classroom Training*. There is a whole section on energizers.

4. **Provide water with lemon, skip the coffee.**
   Do your best to not have coffee available in the room because that's going to dehydrate Doug even more. Instead, see if you can get lemon water which helps to freshen breath, flush toxins from the system, and wake the body up.

5. **Provide snacks.**
    Just in case Doug hasn't had carbs yet, provide snacks in the room. Skip the bagels and choose bananas, eggs or oatmeal. If you are a conference planner, make these available starting day two of the conference as part of the breakfast and your speakers will thank you.

6. **Provide multiple, shorter breaks.**
    Instead of doing a longer 15-minute break, opt for three 5-minute breaks. Or choose to do 7-minute breaks. This will give Doug a chance to throw water on his face in the bathroom or walk around a bit. You are still giving learners their 15-minute break but in segments that are more useful for a bad hangover. Let learners know toward the beginning that you plan to do more breaks that are shorter in duration.

7. **Keep small group discussions under two minutes.**
    Keep timing in your head and shorten discussions to help with focus. Consider using 30-, 60- or 90-second discussions instead. If Doug is actually drunk, he may blabber on and on, and you want to avoid that.

8. **Private conversation.**
    Most times you'll find that the hungover person tries to hide it or attempts to cover it up with a lot of cologne or perfume. Doug may attempt to be an overly good participant. But there are times when the individual is still drunk and his conduct is poor. Take a minute to pull Doug aside and let him know that you know. Let him know you expect better participation and behavior and don't want to remove him from class. Ask if he thinks he is able to do that or if he is too sick and needs to go home.

9. **Document the incident.**
    If all else fails and Doug's behavior continues even after a private conversation, write down what has occurred. You may want to have someone else in the room sign the document as a witness. This helps

human resources. Although it's typically the manager's position to do so, management may not have been in the room and witnessed the contact for themselves.

10. Notify Doug's manager.

Share the incident with the manager and see what the manager would like to do about it. Follow the guidance the manager provides.

11. Remove the participant.

If the behavior continues after the manager was notified, privately ask Doug to go home and come back for day two of the session better prepared. It does not need to be a long conversation; in fact, the shorter the better. If he refuses, remind him that you gave him a warning earlier, and it's time for him to go home and get well. Maintain a kind heart with a helping versus disciplinarian tone for better success.

The Introvert

"I'll just sit in the back and hopefully nobody will talk to me."

Someone could get away with that at most conferences, but they'd be in for a surprise at The Bob Pike Group. BPG's mantra is "the person doing the talking is the person doing the learning." That's such a tried and true principle of learning that BPG consultants never lecture longer than ten minutes between interactive activities.

Do group games, partner projects, and teach-backs sound like an introvert's worst nightmare? To some people, yes! Approximately thirty percent of your audience may prefer a more private, quiet, and contemplative environment. Thank goodness there are ways to design interaction and honor introverts at the same time! It's a fun challenge when you have the right tools.

Try these strategies to help your introverts, like Shy Sharon, find their place in class. They will have more fun and confidence and will walk away with a better taste in their mouths because you tailored it just for them.

1. **Provide self-reflection time.**
   Providing time to think on one's own reenergizes the introvert. Give Sharon a chance to breathe and take in the information. Introverts aren't necessarily reflective learners, but they do appreciate doing a self-reflective exercise on the content that was learned. Journaling and brainstorming on one's own allows for them to not only make sense and meaning of the content but recharge at the same time.

2. **Individual learning exercises.**
   Think of ways you can make your interactive learning individualized. This could include pre-work that's done in micro-learning, or very small segments, like viewing a flashcard, reading a paragraph, or answering a question, or work in the class. Consider having an action planning page, templates to fill in with their content, or a practical application that can be done on their own. The wallflower appreciates when you assign a chapter of a book to read versus reading as a small group. If you have materials that include marketing pieces that need to be read, allow learners to do it on their own and then share their insights with their partners or small groups.

3. **Provide choices.**
   Oftentimes trainers give instruction and direction with only one option. It just comes naturally to tell learners what to do. Next time, consider allowing learners to either work in partners or alone, work inside the room or outside the room, enjoy lunch with friends or on their own, or allow them to create a skit that covers the same information. Choices will allow your different types of learners opportunity to take in information the way they learn best or enjoy most.

4. **Follow the safety scale.**
   This is true for all types of difficult participants. The one end of the safety scale says it's always safest to work by oneself. There's no need to meet someone new, struggle to maintain a conversation, or say something that they are unsure about. It's safest to think by oneself. When doing small-group discussions, consider allowing learners to

think for a minute alone before they provide their thoughts to their group.

The second safest is working with a partner. There's comfort in just sharing your ideas and getting feedback from one individual. Over time, introverts become comfortable with their partners, so consider sticking with the same learning partners for the entirety of the class.

The third safest is working with a small group of people. Stick with five individuals or fewer for best results. Small group work could be discussions, games, brainstorming, product development, et cetera.

The fourth is large group work because it's so public and the introvert could feel uncomfortable sharing in front of a large group. Bob Pike is an introvert but a professional speaker. So there are definitely examples of introverts who are comfortable in a large group, but a majority prefer sharing in a smaller setting.

At the other end of the safety spectrum, which is arguably not safe, is the mystery call-on. This is where you randomly select someone in the room to share. This method will shut down a number of your difficult participants and is not recommended.

5. **Rotate team leaders "randomly."**
Make sure the introvert like Sharon has an opportunity to be a team leader, but make her think it's random. The first few times you call team leaders, you probably do so in ways where you couldn't possibly know who would become leader. For example, who rode a bike last, who took public transportation most recently, who is going on vacation soonest, or who attended a performance of some sort most recently. After having done that a few times and you notice the introvert hasn't chimed in yet, have the next "random" leader be chosen by a physical attribute that makes Sharon the next leader. For example, if she has the shortest hair in her small group, use that. Or if she is the tallest, use that.

6. **Provide additional time.**
It isn't always easy to find extra time for work to be completed, but an

introvert like Sharon will feel blessed to have just a few minutes more where she can reflect on her own.

7. **Show warmth.**
   When talking with the self observer, have warmth in your smile and your mannerisms. A gentle spirit can bring out most quiet people. When connecting with them, there's no need to speak at a fast pace, but instead speak calmly and a bit quieter than what you might be used to.

8. **Use rewards.**
   Praise and encouragement provides intrinsic motivation. Letting Sharon know she has done a nice job interacting can be rewarding enough. You could also provide extrinsic rewards for working so well with partners or in small groups. Everyone might be getting that reward, but it shows the introvert that you appreciate her efforts.

9. **Move the introvert to the front table.**
   Be selective in who is at the table with this individual. Select people who are kind, slightly outgoing and encouraging. Do not put Sharon next to the class clown! The extroverts in the room are a bit too much.

10. **Silent work time.**
    Instead of playing soft music or having participants sit next to one another, allow for silence and learners to move to a space that works for them and away from those loud breathers!

11. **Offline conversation.**
    This conversation is fairly mild. It is simply asking the introvert what you can do to make it a more comfortable session for her. She will likely know what it will take for her to be a bit more engaged and not overwhelmed. Introverts know themselves better than an instructor who has known them for a day. Then do your best to accommodate Sharon's requests. If she says she doesn't want to participate, try to find a solution that will work for her to still get what she needs while still being engaged.

The Know-It-All

"I could have told you that."

The Know-It-All is an over-confident, slightly arrogant, or somewhat cocky person who was sent here from a far, far land to grace everyone else with the benefit of his knowledge. Okay, that's a little harsh.

Know-it-alls are also excited about the content, passionate about their experience, and eager to showcase their ideas. They like stickers and buttons and points—the more the better. They raise their hands, even before the question is completed, because they have another tip for everyone at the tip of their tongues.

Nobody should be the sage on the stage in learning and development. Training works best when more people share their experience, contribute ideas and engage with the content. One talking head—no matter how good the ideas—in the long run stifles learning for everyone else.

Level-set your class and nip know-it-alls in the bud to make training the best it can be. Here are simple ideas to do just that without anyone feeling corrected or handled along the way.

1. **Allow pre-tests or testing out.**
   Oftentimes everyone is sent to class because that's just what's done. If you begin to notice a know-it-all who won't give up, consider asking if he could test out and provide this as an option to this individual. If he takes the test and fails, he now knows that maybe he needs to learn something. If he passes, you're the joy of the class that is missing one wise guy.

2. **Identify the problem.**
   As you begin to see the know-it-all, figure out what the problem is. Could it be the activities are a bit too easy? Or maybe she is taking over the conversations at her table with too many "I think" ideas. Once you've figured out what is happening, come up with a solution to minimize the impact on others. If she is taking over conversations, perhaps use the "winds of fate" solution. From time to time, randomly, the "winds of fate" blow in and take away the voices of one participant per table. Ironically, it's going to be the know-it-all at their table.

3. **Honor experience.**
   Take the time to actually listen to what she is saying. She may actually have some valid insight and knowledge on the topic. Once you've judged her a smart aleck, this can be hard to see, but attempt to see the best in her. From time to time, have the team leader be the person who has the most experience with the topic or allow the know-it-all to share a story or example with the rest of the group. Not too many people enjoy hearing from the windbag all the time, so make sure to honor her in quiet ways as well. This could be offline by sharing how impressed you are with the amount of knowledge she already has on the topic and how grateful you are she is here to learn even more.

4. **Put them to work.**
   Just like the hijacker, it's time to take the know-it-all to task. Put him to work as a scribe, the person who hands out materials, or perhaps a manual laborer moving tables or flip chart stands and the like. Since he "already knows the info," he will not be missing much. He may

find himself struggling a little later on because he missed something, but he won't admit it and will find a way to figure it out. After all, the know-it-alls are typically pretty smart.

5. **Intermittent eye contact.**
   Keep coming back to her eyes to let her know that you're paying attention to her and keeping an eye on her. Don't stare at her because that becomes awkward for the whole group. Instead share one or two sentences while looking at her, and then look away and come back to her again a couple of minutes later.

6. **Change partners.**
   Think about that last lunch you had with the friend who can't stop talking. You know the one where you walk away thinking, "Why do I do this to myself?" That is how all of the other participants, and perhaps even you, might be feeling after just listening to this person for a couple of minutes. Instead of having a consistent learning partner the entire session, rotate partners so no one person is "stuck" listening to the know-it-all for the entire class.

7. **Rotate groups.**
   Just like changing partners, it's also important to change groups. If you have a two-day course, change small groups at least three times. This way, learners know they will only be at this table for a couple of hours. Other participants are very grateful when you say it's time to rotate tables. Instead of being annoyed by the movement, they're excited for the swap.

8. **Establish group questioning.**
   The hijacker is to objecting or belittling what the know-it-all is to not listening because there is nothing to learn. Both need this technique. When he asks a question that is clearly just showing how smart he is, have each table share their answers to the half-question. Having peers at his table share their thoughts is a great way to squelch the all-knowing individual. Continue to use this method every single time

Know-It-All decides to take the stage. Pretty soon his peers are going to tell him to stop, which allows you to maintain your stance and keep respect versus having the individual upset with you. Oftentimes the know-it-all cares more about what his peers think than what the instructor thinks.

9. **Rotate team leaders.**
After using this technique to get the introverted to talk, you'll use this technique for the opposite purpose: to get the know-it-all to not talk. Pick a team leader who will definitely not be the know-it-all. Then assign the task of sharing first to the team leader. In the 30, 60, or 90 seconds of the conversation, only one or two people will be able to share. You know that the team leader will be one of those two. Leave it up to the group as to who gets to be second. At least you hear from one other individual should the know-it-all decide she is going to say something again.

10. **Deflect comments.**
Do not let your training get railroaded by this person. Quickly acknowledge his statement with a "thanks for the suggestion." Do this each time he pulls you aside to give you feedback or shares his idea in class. It's quick, and it helps you move on.

11. **Use facts and research.**
When someone thinks she knows so much, it's your job to help her see other resources could be helpful. One way to do this is to cite your sources, the research behind the content. It is hard to argue with the facts.

12. **Ask questions.**
Keep small group discussions short as often as possible. Sixty-second discussions or less typically means only one person shares, and you can select a team leader, other than the know-it-all, to begin the conversation or share his or her idea first. This way others have a chance to share insight. One easy way to do this is to number off every

person one through five at each table. Let the participants know that the person who has the number one at your table will be the team leader first, and you will move through all five. Each time you have them share their ideas and thoughts, use the same directions and have another person at the table write the ideas on the whiteboard. If the team leader doesn't have an answer, example, insight or story to share on the topic, let the participants know that they are always welcome to ask the table or one other individual to assist.

13. **Offline discussion.**
    Isaac Asimov said, "People who think they know everything are a great annoyance to those of us who do." Clearly Asimov dealt with some of the same people we do today! It is not our job to decide if the know-it-all really does or does not know what she is talking about, but it is our job to offer constructive feedback on her behavior. Attempt to get her to agree to whatever the solution might be. It is best if the learner and you come up with the solution together versus you just telling her what to do. By doing this, there is more buy-in and follow-through. In some cases, she doesn't even know that she has been coming across as a know-it-all, so we don't want to embarrass her. Consider this offline discussion exploratory.

14. **Post quotes around the room.**
    The human brain goes into a trance about thirty percent of the time. Knowing this, you want learners to take their mental break in your world. Posting quotes around the room is a quiet way of getting messages across all throughout the day, so some of these could easily pertain to know-it-alls.

    For example:

    a. Issac Asimov said, "People who think they know everything are a great annoyance to those of us who do."
    b. African proverb—"A wise man never knows all; only fools know everything."
    c. "Unless you are Google, stop acting like you know everything."

15. Challenging activities.

When doing partner or group work, give the know-it-all's group the most difficult task to accomplish. Keep him at the top of his game. Give him the opportunity to stretch what he already knows and take it to the next level. Sometimes difficult personalities show up when things are too easy.

16. Agree to disagree.

If she continues to push back with her wisdom, but it is different from what you're teaching, take a moment to share that it's best you agree to disagree. Keep it to just that so you don't open yourself up to a long conversation later on. If she does come up to you later to reiterate her point, let her know that, although you see her passion, it is best to lay this to rest and agree to disagree.

The Latecomer

Each time Chick-fil-A opens a new restaurant, people camp out overnight in a cult-like following to be among the first 100 customers. The reward: free chicken sandwiches for a year! Or consider how many people walk into a Broadway play or musical after the curtain goes up. At $300 a head for *Hamilton*, not too many people show up late.

People are early or on time when they care. Sometimes they care because of the reward, like free chicken; other times they care because of the pain, like wasting money. Likewise, people are more likely to run late when reward and pain are absent from the equation.

The following are ideas you can implement to make your training sessions anticipated events, kind of like *Hamilton* or a Chick-fil-A grand opening!

1. **Anticipate latecomers.**
   Although your welcome letter is very clear that the start time is 8:30 a.m., for some, that means leaving the house five minutes before in hopes of not running into traffic. Assume this is going to happen, and in your letter, overcome it by saying donuts will be served at 8 a.m.,

and we start promptly at 8:30. Or tempt them with something else for the half hour before start time should you know what your audience prefers. Maybe that's a game in the back of the room or working on a puzzle. By having something going on for 30 minutes prior to start, there's an incentive to get there slightly before the class begins.

2. **Start on time, end on time, be on time.**
It's your job as the trainer to model what good looks like. Be present and ready to go with all of your technology and posters 15 minutes before class begins. Then you have the last 15 minutes for greeting people. During the training, as you look at the clock and you notice time is ticking down, consider taking off a piece of content or two. The best thing you can do is watch your pacing the entire time so that this doesn't occur, but if it does, you're better off covering those two pieces the next day or not at all.

3. **Keep an open seat near the door.**
I've heard some trainers make late arrivers walk all the way to the back of the room past everyone else to get to a seat. Instead of embarrassing them from the get-go, when you see a couple of participants won't make it in time, reserve a seat at the front tables for them. Guilt and shame shouldn't come from the front of the room; these have no place in the classroom at all. Try honey, not vinegar, instead, and you will make friends. Friends trust, respect, and desire to please one another. You are in a much stronger position when being respectful to others.

4. **Ignore last-minute arrivers.**
Instead of making a snide remark like, "Thank you for finally joining us," ignore the belated and continue on with the content. This is far more honoring to those in the classroom on time, which should be your goal.

5. **Use a common clock.**
Sometimes tardiness is simply because someone's clock is off. To avoid this, share with the class before break that "my phone says 10:45; feel

free to change yours to the correct time!" This typically gets a chuckle, and it lets the delayed folk know that time is of the essence.

6. **Use specific, unique times.**

    Sometimes people are late because they don't pay attention to the time, thinking that their "gut" will tell them when time is up. Use times other than five, 10, or 15 minutes for break. People think they know how much time that is. Instead use odd times like 11 minutes or 14 minutes. Somehow, unconsciously, we realize we don't really know how long 14 minutes is, so we had better set a timer. Do the same with lunch. Instead of 60 minutes, try 58 minutes or 62 minutes.

7. **Use learning partners.**

    Having a partner to whom you are accountable increases responsibility. The latecomer may not respect your time but may respect the time of a peer. Prior to break, let the participants know that when they come back in 14 minutes, they'll go straight into a partner activity so "please be back on time so your partner doesn't have to do this alone." By letting them know what's to come, it may motivate them to be back for their new friends.

8. **Reward on-time behavior.**

    When time is up, rewards can go out immediately. Say something like, "Thanks for being back on time. Give yourself a point for being here and another point if your entire table is back." You could also put them right into a fun "do-now" activity. These are quick activities that can be done alone or in a competitive fashion for even more points. Competition is a motivator and when the behind-time participants arrive and see what's going on and that it happens whenever they are back late, it will make them start to think twice about delaying their arrival. If their table missed out on a point because of their tardiness, oftentimes tablemates will tell the tardy to be back on time next time as they don't want to lose points.

9. **Offline conversation.**

   In this private conversation, ask questions about why that learner is repeatedly late. Resist making assumptions and instead let her share with you what her struggle is. Once she has shared, ask if there is something she could do to overcome that struggle or a way that you could help. Share from the place of serving and helping, not grumbling or complaining.

The Petty Rule Breaker

There are rule followers and rule breakers. The latter truly think rules don't apply to them as long as they have a good reason. Rule breakers park in the no-parking zone even when the lot is empty because they aren't likely to be in anyone's way. And they set cruise control to five miles per hour over the speed limit on purpose because five miles doesn't bother anyone, not even officers!

In class, petty rule breakers are the last ones in their seats thirty seconds after the break ended. They check their phones one more time after you call it a screen-free zone. They flip ahead in the workbook and fill in blanks!

Petty rule breakers have a way of getting under a trainer's skin, but the situation can be handled without rule breakers realizing it if you use these tips.

1. **Establish ground rules with the class.**
   Perhaps you already have ground rules on the floor when people enter, but Rule Breaker Ray doesn't think it applies to him. It's time to establish ground rules with the class. Have participants share what

makes a great learning environment and write it on one flip chart. On a second flip chart, write what they say hinders their learning. After the lists have been compiled, say, "Please stand if you agree to do your best not to do these things [point to the list that hinders] and your best to do the things on this list like: …[List off the things that the group put on the second chart so they hear it one more time]."

Let the group know that if they remember other things later in the day, they can add it to either list. However, they will need to ensure the rest of the group knows it has been added. Once they have all stood up, say, "Thank you for making this an environment where everyone can learn optimally. If you notice someone accidentally breaking one of the rules on the hinder list, just kindly let them know."

If there's someone that did not stand up, ask "With what item on these lists are you struggling?" This gives him the opportunity to share what is challenging for him and gives an opportunity for the class to overcome it with the person.

2. **Post "random" quotes around the room and refer to them.**
"Integrity is doing the right thing, even when no one is watching," wrote C.S. Lewis. This quote is one of many you could have around the room. From time to time, make those posters a talking point. Don't wait until the petty rule breaker has broken the rules many times. Instead, start from the very beginning so Ray thinks it is part of class. Head to the posters that you've put up about rule breaking when you start to see this behavior.

3. **Model good behavior.**
Apply the Pygmalion effect. This is basically the golden rule that says treat others as you would want to be treated. If this petty rule breaker is treated with respect, in return he will begin to treat others with respect. When spoken to in a polite and gracious manner, participants will do the same.

4. **Reward expected behavior intermittently.**
    When someone is given a reward every single time they do what you want them to, it becomes expected. Class time shouldn't be spent constantly handing out rewards; rewards should instead be randomly awarded throughout the day. The randomness means you don't have to remember to do it every time. You can simply say, "You all have done such a wonderful job staying focused, being on time, and encouraging one another! Everybody, roll the die on your table, and that's how many points each of you will receive. Good luck!" What a fun way to be rewarded! Now it becomes a game, and no one is the wiser.

5. **Limit the impact on others.**
    Because the petty rule breakers are not as obtrusive as the fighter or the know-it-all, sometimes they fly under the radar for a period of time. But when you begin to see Rule Breaker Ray quickly checking his phone, texting, looking at his smart watch and checking his text messages, begin to walk over to his table while you are talking. Just your presence helps to limit the impact on others.

    If the behavior doesn't stop, the next time you have the group in an activity, whisper to Ray that his behavior is becoming a distraction to others, and it would be helpful if he could put his phone away and on a mode where it doesn't pop up on his watch. Let him know that he will have plenty of breaks so he can keep up with his work, and share that you really appreciate his cooperation. Then make sure that you do give an extra break.

6. **Utilize group accountability.**
    If you established ground rules on the two flip charts earlier in the day, refer back to them later in the day after lunch or a break. Say, "I believe everyone came to this class ready to learn today. But sometimes we might be doing things on this list, and it can be a distraction to others. Throughout the day, if you happen to notice someone else doing one of these things, this is a safe place to quietly let one another know. Sometimes we do not even know when we are doing something

distracting. If you're uncomfortable saying something, give your peer an extra point, and let him or her think through what distracting behaviors he or she might be doing." This works best if you have physical tickets or stickers or something like that so learners can just give that item to one another as a quiet reminder.

7. **Create a positive and fun environment.**
   When people are having fun and are engaged, difficult behaviors go down. Notice the activities that get your students energized and excited, and repeat similar types of activities. I don't mean identical activities, because we want to have variety, but I do mean the same concept. You may notice that the competitive relay race of knowledge you did before lunch was well received and decide to do another competitive activity in the afternoon. Making your classroom a fun, laid-back and positive place diminishes poor behaviors and leaves room for you to be able to say something to Ray and keep him on track.

8. **Acknowledge and praise expected behavior authentically.**
   When you notice that someone is genuinely trying to break a bad habit, be sure to thank him at an appropriate time. If you had whispered in his ear earlier about the behavior, find a time to say, "I have noticed how hard you work to limit XYZ behavior and want to thank you." As long as you are sincere and can truthfully say something of the sort, make a point to share encouragement even with small wins.

9. **Apply the two sister stations, WII-FM and MMFI-AM.**
   What's In It For Me and Make Me Feel Important About Myself are the two sisters stations at work that can help the rule breaker turn his act around. Allowing time for individuals to figure out what they want to get out of the next section or share what their biggest takeaways were not only helps the transfer of training but also keeps the rule breaker from finding other things to do.

   How can you make learners feel important about themselves? Try using their first names, allowing them to share their story, earnestly listening to them when they're talking to you, and showing consideration. Find ways that are comfortable for yourself and work with your audience without being patronizing. If you have a rough and tough group, don't go all mushy-gushy on them.

10. **Create concrete exercises.**
    With this particular difficult participant, be sure the rules are clear and set expectations. There shouldn't be room for creativity in the majority of your exercises. If you aren't specific in the desired outcome, the petty rule breaker will find a way to deliver something other than what you wanted. For instance, if Rule Breaker Ray needs to work alone in silence, specifically say that or if you want a poster with more than one color on it, say that too. Know what good looks like and how to get that point across.

11. **Have an offline conversation.**
    Don't ignore violations; rather revisit or share expectations. Typically this individual does not need another lecture or to be sent to his manager or HR. Rather, he needs a simple conversation about what you expect for the next half day or the remainder of the class. Remember to have him come up with a solution on how he can make that happen. Then you are able to hold him accountable to what he decided. Keep this conversation light and short. It's a gentle reminder versus the reprimand. This conversation can backfire on you if you demand a change in his behavior. By demanding, you're likely to get the exact opposite of what you were desiring and have a bigger problem on your hands. Use the offline conversation as a final resort.

The Preoccupied

Have you ever driven around town on auto-pilot and suddenly wondered how you got to where you were? Such is the problem with pre-occupation. The mind is competing for too many pieces of your life at one time, and important details are bound to get missed.

A technology firm recently brought together employees from all across the country for an important summit. The problem was, while one person was up front talking, everyone else was someplace else, courtesy of the World Wide Web. Literally nobody was engaged in this expensive, important meeting.

In training, people are punched in for class but out to lunch in their heads. They are too busy making grocery lists, checking email, and shopping on Amazon to keep up with your PowerPoint presentation. Don't give up—instead, try these steps before and during training to help everyone in the room, especially Preoccupied Patty, be there in body and mind!

1. **Limit distractions.**
   Sit and think for a moment about what helps you stay focused when there is a sea of chaos around you. Help Patty by removing some of the distractions for her. Turn down the music in the classroom. If you're showing a video, slightly dim the lights to better focus on the scene you're showing. If you normally have thirty posters on the walls, try taking a few down after lunch, leaving up only the ones that are used for revisiting.

2. **Clear off tables.**
   If you have a lot of things on the tables, at break time, have teams bring up the extra items that are not necessary. Fewer items mean fewer distractions for Patty who will then be better able to focus on content. If you normally give three white board marker choices, make it one. Have poster markers next to the posters instead of on the tables. Take a minute or two and have the learners pick up their garbage and dirty plates and put them away.

3. **Engage learners in pair shares.**
   Having the preoccupied connect with just one individual provides them with a high level of attention. When giving directions for the paired work you will be doing, remind them to stay focused and on task as they only have a limited amount of time to complete the conversation or the work. Preoccupied Patty's partner will be motivated to do as you have asked which in turn helps her keep Patty focused.

4. **Use small group discussions.**
   Small groups are a great way to re-engage someone who is wayward like Patty. Make Patty the team leader and give her the job of taking notes and reporting back out. She will be forced to focus on the conversation and be ready to share instead of doing something else. Sneaky, isn't it?

5. **Re-engage using physical and mental energizers.**
   The real goal with the preoccupied is to continually reengage them back into what you're teaching. Having learners stand up and stretch or do a learning puzzle at their table redirects Patty's attention and gets her back on track without you having to say anything. It also helps the rest of the room re-engage as well. Physical energizers are done standing up and include giving high fives, moving around, or other active exercises. You could also do a walking lecture. Don't go anywhere too exciting otherwise their brains will go somewhere else. But walking the halls in a quiet area can help redirect their thinking.

   Mental energizers that require using both sides of the brain can also be done standing up. It could be a word puzzle, a number puzzle or a Rubik's cube. Don't spend a lot of time on your physical or mental energizers because, when you have a preoccupied person in your classroom, you're going to need to increase the number of times you work to re-engage them.

6. **Ask direct questions.**
   Without getting into the mystery call-on, where you suddenly ask an individual a question he or she doesn't know how to answer because he or she was distracted, ask the individual like Patty a question you know she knows the answer to. When was the last time Patty was paying attention and ask a broad enough question she can answer it no matter what. Remember, the idea is to re-engage and re-direct attention back to the front of the room, not embarrass Patty.

7. **Use proximity.**
   As you may have seen in prior chapters with the other difficult participants, walking closer to this individual helps to quickly re-engage them. If Patty is so distracted she doesn't notice you right next to her, "accidentally" bump her chair or knee as you walk by as a covert way of gaining her attention.

8. **Be unexpected.**
   Create curiosity whenever possible. Do not let the learners know

what's around the corner. Instead, do something surprising! Suddenly have each table select someone to do a dance-off or stop mid-sentence and share a riddle. Be sure to let the group know that it is on purpose, that you are trying to keep them on their toes and that they never know what might happen. By sharing your rationale, you will look creative, not spacey.

9. Use humor, not jokes.

Another easy way to regain the attention of the distracted is to be part standup comic with the content. If you can find a way to throw in a funny line here and there, that's great! If you're not humorous, ask the room to come up with a funny way to describe something they learned that day. It's a great way to revisit and get the group laughing. The preoccupied do not want to miss a good laugh. When everyone else is laughing and they missed the joke, the preoccupied realize that multitasking isn't an actual skill of theirs. And because they don't want to miss more, they stay tuned for a bit longer.

10. Provide quick technology breaks.

Technology is one of the biggest distractions, so why not do a two-minute tech break? This meets many learners' needs and desire to be social online, and because they know you will provide these short breaks, they can keep their phones in their pockets or purses. When they know you'll do several of these throughout the day, they are far more likely to comply when you ask them to put their phones away until the next break. You could even ask participants to tweet out something they have learned or take a picture and post a one-line description of what they learned to Instagram.

The Prisoner

Think back to your time in high school. Did you ever have detention? It wasn't a happy place. It was mandatory, regulated, and totally against your will. Because of a mandate from a higher authority, you lost your choice and sense of control for that hour, and you were forced to sit in a room with people you didn't want to be with, counting the minutes. Wait, are we still talking about detention? Depending on who you ask, this scene could also describe how some people feel about mandated company training.

You've seen the Prisoner before. His boss made him attend your class. If she wasn't forced, she'd be anywhere but in your room. The Prisoner shows you with body language, maybe even tells you, "I need to be here, but I sure don't need to enjoy it!"

Winning over the Prisoner is one of the most rewarding experiences a trainer can have. Here are some of the quickest, easiest ways to make that happen.

1. **Name the elephant in the room.**

    Prisoners are your special project. They're one of the most difficult types of people in your room. If you teach mandatory training, it is likely you've met this type of person before. They make you work harder to do your job, and oftentimes it is a thankless one.

    If you know your audience is walking in with a prisoner attitude, then let them gripe for 30 seconds. Seriously, tell them, "For 30 seconds, talk at your tables about all the things you'd rather be doing than being here in this course." They will be surprised and know that you are no fool.

    After they've taken their 30 seconds, do not ask them to share what they came up with. Rather tell them, "Now take the next two minutes to come up with a list of the benefits of being here. Your team leader and scribe is the person who got the most sleep last night. Since we all get to be here today, let's find ways to make the best of the situation."

    I give them two minutes because it takes them awhile to come up with anything. After time is done, solicit answers back from the team leader. After they share, thank them, acknowledge that some may feel the training is a waste of time, but that you're glad they found something to get out of the day anyway. This allows them time to find a "what's in it for me" element to the class. I don't have them do this on their own because some of them wouldn't find anything, but by hearing their peers, they might take something away.

2. **Use group dynamics.**

    For the prisoner, allow their peers to come to your aid. When there's a question, have their tables answer it. Whoever said there's no such thing as a dumb question clearly wasn't a teacher because prisoners come up with them all the time! You'll tell them how long break is and, just before you put them on break, the prisoner will ask, "How long is break?" Although you literally just told the group 30 seconds ago, resist telling the prisoner the answer, and instead have his table share the answer. After he has asked his table three pointless questions, and you used the same methodology of having his table answer, his tablemates will ask him to pay better attention and oftentimes tell him to stop asking stupid questions.

3. **Build a relationship.**
    Make time to connect with the prisoner one-on-one, whether it be at break, lunch, or during an exercise or activity. Find ways to build a bridge through common interests or disinterests. If they say they love heavy metal, and you prefer classical, instead of saying, "I don't like heavy-metal," try "No way! My neighbor plays in a heavy metal band, and I've had the chance to see them play a couple of times." Notice how you just built a bridge instead of complaining about your neighbor who plays his heavy metal too loudly? Both statements are true, but one builds a bridge and the other is insignificant to this person. By listening more than you speak, your relationship can build, and the prisoner's armor comes down. If you have multiple prisoners, make an effort to reach each one throughout the day. As you win one over, the others follow more quickly, so you may want to start with the easiest prisoner to win the hardest ones over more quickly.

4. **Rotate the team leader.**
    Don't let the prisoner be a leader all the time and voice his opinions too often. The "wah-wah-wah" of his whining voice will get overbearing. When you switch up who leads the group, you are both minimizing the impact of the prisoner and controlling his behavior.

5. **Switch tables.**
    If you haven't yet won over the prisoner, take the time to switch the tablemates after about two hours. The person sitting directly next to this individual is exhausted and starting to become a prisoner herself. You don't want all of your audience members to be taken captive by your prisoner and turn on you. Casually switch groups and move on. One easy way to switch is to have all participants grab one of the five different colored markers on the table. Then tell them all the greens are at one table while all reds are at another table, and so on.

6. **Use proximity.**
   To keep a better eye on this individual when he is working in small groups or doing wall work, stick close to him. Make sure he is not derailing the exercises and activities but instead staying focused and engaging appropriately. If you find that he is not behaving, this is a good time to pull him aside and ask him briefly how he is doing. This continues to build a relationship between the two of you and lets him know that you care. Keep the conversation quick so he isn't away from the activity too long.

7. **Carry on.**
   Sometimes the best thing to do is just keep moving through the content versus making a big deal out of something that may be small. When the prisoners get on your nerves, the little things can seem big. Take a moment to consider whether to make a big deal out of it or to continue moving forward. By moving forward, you are respecting the remainder of the class and not giving attention to the one who doesn't want to be there anyway.

8. **Share examples that are real.**
   Know your content well enough to be able to use examples that are true to their world. Use examples that are recent from the company, or ask them to share with one another an example of how they have seen this content used back on the job in the past six months. Make that a small group activity because not everyone may have experienced what you're talking about. This helps them make connections to their world, allows them to learn from one another, and helps them see that what you're teaching really does occur or apply.

9. **Ask them for their help.**
   To continue building a relationship, ask the prisoner to help you. It could be something small like taking lunch orders or could be as simple as handing out some materials. The real reason you're asking the prisoner for further assistance is to gain her trust and respect. When people respect you, they begin to follow.

10. Focus on others.

If you're having a hard time breaking the prisoner, focus on others in the room. Because you want to be fair, you should be doing this already, but sometimes you have invested so much energy into trying to get that prisoner to "flip," you have forgotten about the rest of the room.

If needed, keep a list of all participants, and check off when you have had a conversation with each one or when you take the time to see if everything makes sense to them. Everyone should have a bit of your time and the other participants appreciate that just because a prisoner is the loudest doesn't mean she is the only one getting attention.

11. Offline conversation.

Ah yes, the dreaded offline conversation. This is not a fun one to have in class because no matter what you say, the prisoner will continue to debunk or push you. Be firm but fair, and let him know his behavior is disrupting the class. Make it about his colleagues and peers versus about you. Focus on the behavior versus them as a person.

You might say, "When off-handed comments are made about the content, it takes at least a minute for your peers to refocus. This takes a lot of time away from their ability to learn. I can see why it might be difficult for you to be in class today. Moving forward, please keep your comments to yourself so that others might have the best chance to absorb the information. What can I do to help you reach this goal?"

Although you may have heard that it's important for both you and the prisoner to come up with a solution, this is one participant who oftentimes flat out refuses to come up with anything. Save your breath and instead just tell him what good looks like. Don't let him walk all over you. Let him know what the consequence will be if it happens again. That means you need to think up what will happen when, not if, he does it again.

12. Manager conversation.

If the prisoner continues to disrupt the class, allow the class to take a break and call the prisoner's manager. Ask her for insight into this individual and if there is anything she knows that really works with him or her that you could apply. Also, ask the manager's opinion about removing the prisoner from class if you deem it necessary. Let her know that is not your goal, but if nothing else works, ask if this would be an acceptable last resort.

BONUS: Scream at the prisoner, slam the door until the glass breaks, and throw things. Then you will get fired and won't have to deal with the prisoners anymore.

The Sleeper

One day, a woman sent her pastor a thoughtful note, thanking him and desiring to encourage him. The last line of the note said, "I especially appreciate listening to your sermons at night when I'm trying to fall asleep." Just what every speaker wants to hear!

If you've had the occasion to hear snores, grunts, and other noises from a person who's fallen asleep in your class, you might be tempted to take it personally. Don't worry; it's not your fault.

People fall asleep in class just like they fall asleep on noisy trains, in loud movies and in packed first-period freshman seminars. Call it caffeine withdrawal, food coma, or jetlag—there are many reasons people fall asleep that have nothing to do with the person up front talking.

How can you save that person, and those around him, from embarrassment when that happens?

1. **Get moving.**

    Perhaps you are teaching third shift and have tired folks. Or maybe you just have tired folks. This is pretty noticeable as they enter the room and get settled in. Take a minute at the beginning of the session to get the blood flowing and energy going. Start your session with an activity that requires people to stand whether they are working at the wall or doing an activity like Four Corners.

    Four Corners goes like this. Point to each corner while verbally labeling it A, B, C or D. Then give a pop quiz with each question having four choices for answers. Learners "vote" for their answer by standing in the corner that represents the answer they have chosen. It requires a bit of planning because you need to have multiple-choice questions. If you have a class that you teach often, I would even have these at the end of your PowerPoint deck with the answers listed so it's not just auditory recall for them to choose a corner.

    Another, quicker idea is to have Koosh balls and two teams. If you have ten people in training, split them into two teams of five. If you have twenty people in training, split into two separate groups for this activity, with each team in each group having five people. One team will stand on one end of the room while the other team stands opposite them on the other end of the room. Have each member of the team answer a question and then throw the Koosh ball to the person on the opposite side. The other team's first person answers the next question. Once the ball is thrown, that person then runs across the room to the other side to the back of the line. Make sure you have a minimum of ten questions so everyone gets a chance to run. It's quick and fun and gets the blood flowing. Don't make this hard on yourself. It can be a get-to-know-you activity with a little bit of content thrown in. For example, ask the question, "What is your favorite animal?" The next question might be "What is one tool you can use to help you manage a project?"

    If you need something simpler than that, try a quick standing stretch or "bust a move." Turn on some music and tell them to show off their skills. Even if they don't dance, at least they're standing up!

2. **Use standing and physical activities.**
   Lecture if you must but never for more than ten minutes. As often as you are able, have participants get up and move around. If you are going to have them share with someone, simply make them stand up and find someone across the room to share with versus staying seated and connecting with the person next to them. Or create a myth or truth exercise to cover content and have them stand on one side of the room if they think information is a myth and move to the other side of the room if they think it is the truth. Use up to ten questions and assume that each question will take approximately two to three minutes. After each question provide a two-minute lecturette to further explain the concept. When they get back to their tables, reveal the answers on a slide and have them fill in the blanks in their workbooks. If you prefer, you can have them take their workbooks with them to take notes while doing the activity.

3. **Provide cold water.**
   Inside countries and parts of the United States, this is a crazy idea! Don't give up on it yet. Cold water wakes up the body, and shivering does, too. If the class is longer than an hour, try not to offer coffee or caffeine because it is a short-lived spike of energy that leaves you feeling low after.

4. **Play the sad card, not the mad card.**
   If someone is really struggling in your class, pull them aside and ask if everything is alright. Give her an opportunity to share what's going on before making assumptions. After she has shared, empathize and ask how you can help. By playing the sad card, you are keeping the relationship intact, especially if something is significantly wrong. If something is really wrong and she is unable to wake herself up, allow her to take a quick nap in a different room. Sleep learning doesn't work. Tell her to set an alarm and come back in twenty minutes. If the class is compliance and she needs to be there the entire time, encourage her to stand at the back of the room to help her stay awake.

5. **Provide a power break.**
   This would be in addition to the regular breaks you take. This is led by you and lasts three to five minutes. Here are a few ideas to get you started.

   - Lead the group on a quick walk around the outside of the building. If it requires taking an elevator, consider taking a walk around the floor that you are on.
   - If there are a lot of sleepy people in the room, take a quick nap. Let them know they can rest their eyes for the next five minutes.
   - If you know a relaxation technique, perhaps lead the group in a relaxation exercise.
   - Offer a snack break with nuts or bananas offered. This can boost your energy quickly.

   Be creative in your power breaks, and use the time wisely.

6. **Turn up the lights.**
   If you have an option of dimming the lights or having them all the way up, do the latter. The brighter it is in the room, the more difficult it is to fall asleep. Even if it makes it a little more difficult to see the slides, at least learners will be awake and listening.

7. **Vary your voice.**
   It is really easy to fall asleep to a monotone voice. A monotone voice is like a lullaby. Take a minute to see if perhaps you have gotten into a rhythm with your voice and work hard to vary it. Speed up your speech to show excitement, and slow it down to show concern. Use the wide range of your vocal chords to create energy and curiosity for the learner. A curious brain rarely falls asleep.

8. **Open windows or cool down the room temperature.**
   Yes, it may be twenty degrees below zero outside, but it's time to wake up the crowd. You don't need to have the windows open for a long time but long enough to cool the room down a few degrees. It's harder to fall asleep in a cold room. Participants should have brought an

extra layer, and they can put it on if needed. Obviously, opening the windows on a particularly sticky, hot day is not a good idea.

9. **Take a field trip outside.**

    If the weather is good and it has not rained recently, take the classroom outdoors. Find content that's coming up soon that you could teach outdoors. There are several options once you're outside. You can have participants stand and enjoy the weather while you are teaching, or you can have them sit on the lawn. If they sit on the lawn, sit with them. It makes the lesson more conversational and interesting. If there is too much noise or traffic, head back in to finish the lesson. Half of the field trip is the walking to get people reenergized.

10. **Quietly take a break.**

    This doesn't happen often, but when someone falls asleep at the table, consider taking your break early and letting everyone know they need to leave the room for the next fifteen minutes. It will provide this person an opportunity to get the rest she needs, and the change in volume typically wakes up the sleeper. Once she has woken up gently, let her know that you understand and the intention wasn't to embarrass her but to give her a couple minutes of much-needed rest. Let her go on a quick break to freshen up, and then call everyone back in. Resist making a joke like, "Welcome to the land of the living!" Although funny to you and others, it just draws attention to the nap and can be embarrassing. If someone falls asleep at the table, he or she likely has a good reason for it.

Training Difficult People

The Slowpoke

Highways have fast lanes on the left and slow lanes on the right. Well, that is how it's supposed to work, but every now and then, a slowpoke goofs the whole system up.

Unfortunately, most training programs don't have a fast and slow track built in. It is one-size-fits-all. However, as you know, people don't all work and learn at the same pace. Slowpokes get stuck, confused, and overwhelmed when information comes at them too quickly.

If your pace of training is right for about eighty percent of the folks in the room, that is a pretty good rate. You will always have about ten percent out front trying to pull everyone faster. And you'll always have about ten percent dragging behind, maybe even slowing the group down.

Slowpokes can be helped along, and these thirteen ideas work wonders in helping the slower folks keep pace!

1. **Use partners.**
   The plodder needs a push, so partner them up with a pal who has more than a passive pace. It also doesn't hurt if the partner has slightly

more skills and is encouraging. When you have a slow personality in the room, do not leave it to fate to find a good partner. If you are unsure who would make a good partner, have everyone lineup by how quickly they feel they pick up concepts. This is self-proclaimed, and there is no wrong answer. If Herbert, your snail, puts himself in the middle, pair him with someone slightly above him. If Herbert puts himself with the most casual of learners, put him with somebody in the middle. Do not pair him up with one of the fastest learners as this will frustrate them both.

2. **Provide assistance.**
During games, breaks, and activities, spend more time hanging out where Herbert is working, and be ready to provide assistance. Do not hover; rather, casually walk around the room, regularly checking in to see how everyone is doing. If you find that Herbert is behind, consider being his partner for the remainder of the exercise to speed up the pace.

3. **Be organized with agenda and expectations.**
Help the straggler speed up by setting the stage with an agenda and expectations. Let the group know that you plan to move at a certain pace, and it is it each individual's job to do his or her best each step of the way. Let them know that if they don't finish a certain task, they can come back to it on the next work break. If that is not possible, let the group know that half of your break time and half of your lunchtime is dedicated to helping those who may need your assistance, and they can find you in the training room. This way, you can get email done while also being available should they need your help. Let them know that it will be the second half of lunch so you actually get a little bit of lunchtime and downtime for yourself.

4. **Ensure your slowpoke isn't just preoccupied.**
Sometimes our slower individuals are actually preoccupied. You may want to read the chapter on the preoccupied learner for additional ideas.

5. **Make avoidance or non-participation impossible.**
   Let's say Herbert isn't preoccupied and is just trying to get out of participating. Take that option away from him by reducing the amount of lecture you do and increasing the amount of work the learners must do. Regularly have participants work together on a project as a small group, and mix it up frequently.

6. **Praise good behavior.**
   When you see Herbert speeding up his pace and producing good work, let him know that. Praise and encouragement are big motivators and simply saying a few words can help him keep pace for the next section. Keep in mind that it may be that this learner is more methodical and reflective and takes a bit more time to consider concepts and ideas before sharing.

7. **Have Herbert sit close to the front.**
   Keep Herbert close to you to reduce the number of distractions and to increase your ability to casually walk by and check in.

8. **Set up a no-loss class, no penalties.**
   Instead of creating a negative atmosphere where people lose points for not completing work, share that you expect their best, whatever that may be. The key is to reduce tension for the casual learner so that retention can be increased.

9. **Provide written instructions for exercises or activities.**
   The people in the room who are self-proclaimed slowpokes or reflective learners need time to digest instructions and do well when things are written out as well as shared verbally. When appropriate and feasible, add those instructions to the workbook. This way, if the slowpokes didn't capture your quick instructions, they can read for themselves and know what is going on. If you are unable to put it in the workbook for whatever reason, write it up, print it out and make it available for anyone to use.

10. **Handouts with fill-in-the-blanks.**

    If the individual is all-around slow, taking good notes may be difficult for him. Writing out most of the notes for individuals and simply having a few fill-in-the-blanks provides a way for them to keep up. Allow for white space within the handout so the faster learners can take additional notes.

11. **Keep reading level at a fourth-grade level.**

    Strike a balance between readability for those who didn't finish high school and those with advanced degrees. What does that look like? This book is written at an eighth-grade level. This is calculated by word choice, length of sentences, and the number of syllables used in the writing. In order to comprehend the information in this book on the first read, the reader would need eight to nine years of formal education. To determine your text's readability, copy and paste text from it and paste it into an online reader like this one: http://bit.ly/CTP2018A. This tool lets you know what sentences should be re-written more simply. Simplify the complex.

12. **Be patient and authentic.**

    It is okay to take an extra minute here and there to show this individual that you care. Speak slowly and clearly and use encouraging words that are authentic, and the learner will attempt to keep up. He will also appreciate the fact that you gave him an extra moment of time.

13. **Use short activities with evidence of accomplishment.**

    This is like the concept of a quick sale. Every new salesperson wants one quick sale to help bolster his or her confidence in selling the new product or service. Activities that require a short attention span and provide a sense of accomplishment do this for the slower learner. For example, if you have a matching game with thirty terms and definitions, break it down into smaller chunks. Give five at a time, and then reveal the correct answers. After you have explained those five, move on to the next batch of five.

14. Use baby steps.

Let's say you are teaching a presentation skills course. Instead of having participants create and present a ten-minute presentation right off the bat, start with having them share a story with a partner. By breaking things down into baby steps for the class, the slow learner can keep up and feel more confident in the process.

The Texter

Walk into your favorite neighborhood restaurant and chances are you'll see a scene like this: four friends sitting in a booth, staring blankly at screens, texting. Physically, they are together. But in every other way, they are in four different places.

According to Experian, U.S. smartphone owners aged 18–24 send sixty-seven texts per day and receive another sixty-one. That works out to about one text every seven minutes of all waking hours! And it doesn't stop or go on pause just because your training program is interesting.

Your classroom today may feel a lot like the restaurant booth where people are together physically but their minds are in different places. One learner's mind is at home with a leaky pipe and plumber running late. Another's mind is at school with a kid who just lost his retainer in the lunch garbage. One's even back in the office asking for the details about the Anderson account.

Try these tips to build invisible structure into your class and get everybody (and every mind) back in the room.

1. **Ground rules.**
   Knowing we are in the digital age, the very first thing your learners should see as they enter your training room is the poster on the ground with the picture of a cell phone. Next to the phone, it says "Thank you for silencing." If you see a few people not noticing the ground rule as they walk over it at the beginning of class, say, "If you didn't have a chance to sign in, please do so now, and if you stepped right over our ground rules for the day, take a moment to stand up and read them so we are on the same page." This way people can save face and pretend to check-in when really they're reading the ground rules. Be sure to put both tasks in close proximity to one another.

2. **Lead by example.**
   It is tempting to have your own cell phone out as a way to check the time or glance down at a quick text message. If you want your participants to put their phones away, then you need to put yours away as well. If you use your phone for music, place it on the speaker so they know the intent and purpose of the phone. Be sure to put your phone on night mode or sleep mode so it doesn't make any noises or vibrate during the class. If you forget to turn off your phone and it rings, pretend to answer it and say to the group, "That's just a reminder. If you have forgotten to silence your phone, do so now!" Be sure to put yours on silent as well.

3. **Use eye contact.**
   As you begin to notice the texter looking at his phone or smart watch, glance in his direction until he looks up at you. It is like playing chess, and you have moved your first piece toward him. When said texter hides the phone under the table so you won't see it, use eye contact once again to show him he was caught a second time.

4. **Interactivity every 10 minutes.**
   Plan your session with digital natives in mind. Keep lectures to ten minutes or less and increase the amount of interactivity. Using less variety means the texter will get bored and be on her phone again. The

individual you are dealing with is probably in the habit of receiving a text 68 times an hour during waking hours. You are up against a habit. By engaging her in discussions and activities, you can reduce that number significantly. It won't break her habit in just a day or two, but it will give her a better opportunity to learn.

5. **Use proximity.**
The next step is to try keep close tabs on the texter. Do this by presenting from right next to where he is sitting, even if it is not the front of the classroom. Make sure you have the PowerPoint clicker so that you can forward your slides from anywhere in the room. By staying close, it is more difficult for him to text without being completely insubordinate.

6. **Cell phone structured activities.**
The majority of your class will have a smartphone, so plan to use it as part of your interactions to keep them engaged. Perhaps let them research on their phone, let them use their technology as the clicker, have them text a friend about what they have learned and then show their learning partner what they texted.

When using the phone in class, make sure you have a way for participants to be held accountable. Do not be the person who has to check every phone. Instead have learning partners work together on one phone or check in with one another and share what they have found along the way. This works fastest from the front of the room if you say, "Pause your research and share with your learning partner what you have uncovered so far."

You may as well do your evaluation digitally. In order to get 100 percent participation, have them fill out the evaluation before their last break. As their "ticket" to go on break, they need to show you their phone with the "thank you" screen up. This may seem silly, but if you have thirty people in the room, to have accurate data, you will need to have at least twenty-seven of them fill out the evaluation.

7. **Brainstorming via projected image.**
   Randomly select a couple of people to bring their phones up with their research text displayed. Then take a photo of their screen and project it on the screen using Reflector 2, a screen-mirroring app. Have the app on your phone ready to go. It is fun to see them get excited that their text made it up on the screen. And if your texter didn't get it done and wasn't selected this time, he knows for the future he better be ready.

   A couple of websites that can be accessed from their phones which also have suggested uses and activities are wallwisher.com, polleverywhere.com, UMU.com, and todaysmeet.com. For the texter, utilize todaysmeet.com for quick exercises and group sharing. It is a simple-to-use tool and creates curiosity and fun while revisiting the content. Keep in mind that every text message gets posted immediately and is not filtered by you. So warn participants to use G-rated comments!

8. **Email breaks.**
   These breaks are in addition to your regular ones and last only a couple of minutes. This allows your addicted phone user to text a couple of people and check a message or two. Make email breaks short and sweet.

9. **Use FaceTime to have a guest speaker.**
   Using the app Reflector 2 to display your phone screen, FaceTime a subject matter expert (SME) and have him or her be your guest speaker. Allow the SME 10 minutes to make something complex easier to understand. This is a fun way to reengage your audience and keep those digital natives curious.

10. **Video or audio record assignments or instructions.**
    Instead of sharing your directions on a piece of paper or just verbally giving them, give participants the web link to the instructions, the assignment, or a video you've created in advance. It is fun to create four different videos and have each group do a slightly different task. The group will be curious as to what the other messages were and will be more focused to see what they come up with. Use bit.ly, an online

web address shortener, to create a shortened code for them to type in to get to your video. Put this code on a 3x5 card and place one on each table.

11. **Allow "Google translate" for ESOL participants.**
    Just because someone is on a phone doesn't mean it's not for good reason. English speakers of other languages (ESOL) may be using Google translate to figure out what you are saying. If you think this could be a possibility, check with the participant at break and ask if he or she is using the phone to assist with the lesson. If the learner says yes, say, "I'm so glad you feel comfortable doing that. What app do you use? Is there anything I can do to make it easier?" This way you find out the answer in a conversational way, and the learner gets what he or she needs. If the learner lied to you, you are likely to see a reduced amount of texting because he or she was caught.

12. **Politely ask him to leave the room.**
    If the texter continues to text and check texts after you have tried all of the above, casually walk over to him and tell him to take the text or call outside. Remind him that when he comes back into the room, he will need to put his phone away. Most often texters say the text or call wasn't important, and they put the phone away, but if they choose to leave the room, at least they're not distracting others.

13. **Quietly ask them to stop.**
    If after you've asked him to leave the room, he continues with his bad behavior, don't give up. Instead, walk over to him and quietly ask him to stop. It might sound something like, "Thanks for putting that away. It's becoming a distraction to me and others. Again, thank you for keeping it in your bag."

14. **FaceTime one of her friends or parents.**
    WARNING! This can be a bit extreme if you don't know the person well and should only be done when the person who is habitually texting has a sense of humor. Pause the class and ask for the participant

to stand. Ask her if her parents have FaceTime. If she says yes, have her pick one or the other to FaceTime. If she says no, let her make a phone call on speaker phone. Let the participant know that once her parent or friend answers, she needs to share with him or her their secret texting habit. When someone does answer and the participant tells her "secret," it typically gets a laugh from the room and the texter stops the behavior moving forward. If you know the participant well enough, you might use this earlier on in class to make a point in a fun way.

The Time Thief

Some companies have a "no drive-by-shootings" policy, which is a strange way of asking people to plan ahead, ask questions at the right time, and be careful not to sidetrack others from their work. Instead of asking about the Murphy account while someone is trying to have a moment of peace (and dignity) in the restroom, the time thief should be encouraged to hold that thought for a more appropriate time.

Time thieves invade the classroom, too. They ask more than their fair share of questions, they request more ideas than what you've presented before they even attempt to implement the ideas you just covered in class, and they have a sneaky way of asking for a "quick second" of your time during lunch, and before you know it, lunch is over.

The time thief is a freeloader. He will take as much as you will give. And then he'll take just a little bit more. When you encounter a time thief in your seminar, take the following approaches to reset the scene.

1. **Protect breaks and lunch.**

    If there's a time thief around, don't plan on using the bathroom during break or eating lunch. To avoid this scenario, share with the audience that it's time for break and that you'll be available halfway through to connect and answer any questions. By setting the expectation, you have the opportunity to say that you'll be back in seven minutes and happy to connect if someone addresses you at the beginning of break. This way you get at least a small break versus no break at all.

2. **Include a "where-to-go" reference section.**

    Because this person is all for the freebies, create a where-to-go section that provides a lot of free resources to which you can refer them. If your session is on gamification, have fifteen websites with free examples and templates. When they ask for more on a certain topic, have them bring their workbooks up to you and show them the ones you would recommend. This makes the conversation concise and still gives the time thief something.

3. **Redirect back to an activity.**

    This individual is self-focused and may not be aware that he is robbing you and others. If you see this happening during an exercise or an activity, simply ring your chime, refocus the group with a quick instruction, and put them back to work. Doing this re-engages the group and the taker.

4. **Be calm in both temperament and speech.**

    Regardless of how many times the individual connects with you throughout your presentation, deliver the message graciously. Doing this may require you to resist rolling your eyes, giving a slight huff, or using the stop sign gesture with your hand. Model what excellence looks like throughout the workshop. Consider slowing your speech and breathe in slowly as you answer her question. If you're unable to be calm and collected, let her know you'll get back to her in a moment. It is perfectly fine to not answer the question immediately. Simply let her know that now is not the right time to get into that but that you'll be available during break to discuss the question then.

5. **Check in with every participant in the class.**
   Spend time with everyone. Don't let your time get sucked by the individual who is hogging the air time. Just because he raised his hand doesn't mean you need to call on him. Use your sign-in sheet and check off names when you have connected with each person on the list to ensure no one has been missed. By making a concerted effort to reach everyone in the class, your participants feel listened to and are less frustrated with the freeloader.

6. **Set boundaries.**
   Identify activities and areas where you can set time limits and expectations. By having clear boundaries, the freeloader and those around her are better able to hold themselves and one another accountable. When starting an exercise say, "You will have five minutes to work on your own. After that time, I will ring a chime, and you'll have five minutes to work with your learning partner. Each partner will share for two-and-a-half minutes. I will display time to help you stay on track." After the five minutes is done, ring the chime and remind participants of the next portion. Add that the person with the longest or shortest hair will be the first to share. Be sure to pick the time thief's partner as the person to go first as the partner will likely be more conscientious of using only half the time. Use a visual timer projected on the screen so everyone can see where time is at.

   You may also need to set boundaries for how often or how much time you're willing to invest in connecting with them. You can quickly do this when the time thief comes up to you by saying, "Thank you for coming up and connecting with me. I have a phone call to make in two minutes, but what can I help you with until then." Planning ahead can ease your getaway. If the freeloader continues to take, and isn't heeding others, take the opportunity to gently say, "I'm so glad you are participating so well in class. Although you were first in line to talk with me, there are several others I haven't had a chance to connect with much today, and I'd like to make sure their needs are met as well. How does that sound?" If he proceeds with his question anyway, you can give a brief answer and have a way to move onto the next person quickly because the time thief already knows your plan. Those surrounding the time thief are grateful and the time thief will have his needs met, either right then or later in the day.

7. **Give her responsibility.**
   Because this individual is a natural taker, provide opportunities for her to give back to others. Ask her to help you put up charts around the room, clean up tables while you're chatting with her, or prep materials for the next activity. The job doesn't matter so much as the opportunity to give back. Typically time thieves don't even notice what you're doing but are excited to be useful to the teacher and have a few extra minutes of instruction.

8. **Be available 15 minutes before, 30 minutes after class.**
   It's amazing how, even after a full day of training is over, the time thief continues to take. In some cases this can be up to 90 minutes more! In order to avoid this sticky situation, share with the class that you will be ready fifteen minutes before class and half an hour after while prepping for the next day to connect and answer questions. Most participants leave promptly, but if the time thief decides to stay, you now have a way to thank him for helping you set up for the next day while giving him advice.

9. **Bolster her confidence.**
   Much of this can be done on the down low to help meet the time thief's need for attention. Notice the little things she is doing well and specifically share how valuable that will be back on the job. Let her know she has done a good job when she allows others to ask questions or share stories. If the time thief really has done a nice job listening to others, point it out. Reward what you want repeated.

10. Offline conversation.

If the moocher has not stopped mooching throughout the day, and you have a second date planned, kindly ask the participant to connect with you after class. While meeting, praise him for what he's done well and gently confront the learner regarding his behavior. Share that it isn't fair to him or to others. Thank him for his engagement and let him know you're excited for what tomorrow brings. The last thing you want to do is turn the time thief into the defeated.

The Tweety Bird

The social media maven has arrived. Plunked down in the front row, she's already snapped a picture of your opening slide and tweeted it out to the world. And #Tweetybird is just getting started.

Today you face the most media and tech-savvy participants of all time. They have a social way of learning and sharing and a seeming compulsion to check in. They have followers who they feel need to hear from them and see pictures of the wonderful places they visit. They tweet, network, snap, post, game, and selfie frequently.

The digital natives have taken over, and they bring an incredible set of skills, technological aptitude and vast digital footprints. Tap into those capabilities and your influence will extend beyond the classroom.

Use these tips to tap into the power of social media while keeping it from driving your class to distraction.

1. **Implement rules.**
   After you have made it through your opener and the day's agenda, it

is time to squash social media unless you are using it for class. Have your learners brainstorm a list of appropriate ways to use social media during the day. Let them share ways they can use it for educational purposes. These should be put on a poster.

The next step is to ask them how cell phones and social media could distract themselves, others, and the teacher. Again, use their words and write them on a poster. Let them know that you appreciate the tech savviness in the room and want to encourage that in appropriate ways. Let them know you will attempt to build in time for them to use their social media for learning in the ways they have brainstormed.

If you are not tech savvy and do not have the first clue as to how to post on social media, ask who in the room is the most socially connected. Pick one of the people who raise their hands and let him or her know that it is his or her job to find ways for the group to use their social media platforms to revisit content throughout the day. The chosen social media manager will be excited by the task, and you can breathe a sigh of relief.

2. **Have a clock in class.**
You may notice that a lot of classrooms don't have clocks hanging in them anymore. If this is the case in your training room, bring a large numbered digital clock and place it at the back of the room. Let the class know that they no longer need to check their phones for the time! You have taken away the main excuse for checking their phones.

3. **Create a social media poster.**
Having a poster in plain sight with a couple of simple questions may help focus those who have a fixation on checking in.

   a. Do I have a specific, positive reason for posting this at this moment?
   b. Did I successfully change social alert settings and disable all alerts?

4. **Take one-and-done social breaks.**

    Even though two friends may be in the same class, it is likely you will see them sitting next to each other posting on the same social outlet. Your tweetybird may hear them laughing at one of her posts. Why not use this knowledge as an opportunity for a quick learning exercise?

    Have participants take a one-and-done social break by pulling up their favorites sites and sharing a favorite idea they've learned from the day. If you have a varied audience, you may have some participants that have few or no social networks. Let participants know they can either go online or write their favorite idea down on their action idea page in the workbook. Be sure to have a page labeled "action ideas" for them to write on.

5. **Integrate into class.**

    Earlier, you created a list of rules with the class. On break, check in with the social media experts in the room and ask them to connect with you for a couple of minutes. Share with them what the upcoming content is and ask them how they could see it being used on social media. As they come up with ideas, choose one you like and ask that person to be ready to share the idea with the class after break. This takes the burden of technology off of you and places it on someone who is savvy in this area. This allows that person to use his or her skill set, and the tech-savvy are ready to help others in the room. Do the exercise in pairs if the idea requires a smartphone and others don't have one or are not a tweetybird themselves.

6. **Hands-on exercises.**

    When hands are busy working on a project or completing an activity, it is very hard to multitask with phones, not impossible, but more difficult. Yes, you may see a few of your addicts taking pictures of themselves and their projects, but at least they are in your world and excited about what they're working on.

7. **Digital break basket.**

    There may come a point in class where you are noticing several learners using their phones alone. In a jovial tone, let the class know that it is now time for our phones to take a digital break. It's their phones' nap time! Set out a basket and let them place their phones in it. Be careful to not come across as condescending!

A couple of the addicts may push back, in which case, you can tell them they may keep their phones as long as they are put away in purses or backpacks, and they don't come out. Warn them that if the phones do come out, they will need to take a break with all the other phones in the basket and will stay there longer than the others. Say this in a light-hearted manner, but if you do see the phones come out, follow up on your promise, and bring the basket over for them to put their phones in.

8. **Call them out quietly at their table.**
   If the phone break is over and they continue to be on their phones, go over to their tables during an activity, and let them know it is really time to put them away as they have become a major distraction to themselves, you, and others. Let them know that you understand it's hard to put it away, but it's necessary for learning to occur.

9. **Create shared lists or concepts to capture.**
   Create a shared Google list that is open to the class and allows them to post their favorite selfies, sayings, or ideas from the class. This may be an advanced activity for some of your learners. Once again, you will want to partner the experts with the novices and have them help their friend find the Google doc and post a few ideas.

10. **Create a class hashtag.**
    If all else fails and the phones continue to be a problem, ask one of your participants to create a hashtag for your class. But let them know that, by the amount of phone checking you've been seeing, there better be a lot of activity on that Twitter feed by break time if the phones continue to be out. This is not giving up but is instead setting a new expectation that may be more realistic for the remainder of your time. After all, you can't force someone to learn, but you can provide opportunities for them to be more successful.

The Unprepared

"May I borrow a pencil? And a piece of paper? And see a copy of yesterday's notes? Does anyone have a laptop charger? Was I supposed to do that *before* coming today?"

Do you ever wonder how some people trudge their way through life without starving to death, getting lost on the freeway, or being fired from their jobs? If they run their lives like they prepare for your class, they are flirting with disaster.

The unprepared make your job a bit tougher because you've got to make up for some of their deficits. You bring extra materials, accommodate their lack of planning, and give up valuable time because they are not ready. In a way, they don't take training very seriously.

While some people are chronically unprepared, you can help them get back on track without catering to their every need. For example, you can:

1. **Provide materials.**

    It is likely you know someone who regularly leaves things at home or can't find what he or she is looking for despite the item being right in front of them. Do not expect anything different from a class of twenty-five. It is likely there is someone who is just like your sister, daughter, spouse, cousin or friend who leaves everything behind. With that in mind, make sure you bring extra materials for them to be successful for the day. Don't expect them to remember a pen or even a pad of paper. Build it into the cost of the course and feel good knowing everyone will have the tools to be successful.

2. **Explain what "pre-pared" means to you.**
Don't expect learners to know the expectations in your head. Think about what contributions you want the class to make, including what preparedness might look like. Present this in an upbeat manner and ask them if there's anything you didn't think of that should be included. Expectations could be: help your partner remember all tools needed for exercises, keep track of your pen, or leave items you don't want lost in your bag.

3. **Apply the two sister stations, WII-FM and MMFI-AM.**
What's In It For Me and Make Me Feel Important About Myself. These sister stations can help the unprepared turn their act around. Allowing time for individuals to figure out what they want to get out of the next section or share what their biggest takeaways are helps with the transfer of training and keeps the dismally unprepared from finding other things to do.

How can you make someone feel important about themselves? Try using his first name, allow her to share her story, earnestly listen when he is talking to you, and show consideration are a few ideas. Find ways that are comfortable for yourself and work with your audience without being patronizing. Oftentimes, those who are unprepared have big hearts and desire to do well. Find the good amidst what's driving you crazy.

4. **Use personal goal setting.**
If the pattern of unpreparedness continues, insert this exercise. Have

participants pick something that they are struggling with and come up with a goal for themselves. Mention "if you're having a hard time being prepared for each exercise, create a goal around that; if you're struggling with using your phone too much, that could be a good goal, or maybe you're preoccupied with something else. Write a goal to try to bring yourself back to learning so you can be ready for our next segment."

5. **Set time limits with a visual timer.**
   The unprepared can easily lose track of time. Help them by being specific with how much time they have to do something and project a digital timer that counts down, so they can see just how much time they have left.

6. **Utilize interactive activities.**
   By keeping the class engaging and using partners or small group work, the unprepared are more likely to keep up and have the tools they need with them because others in the group hold them accountable. When choosing a team leader for your activities, allow the unprepared to take their turns being the leader. This gives them a moment to shine and will definitely keep them on task and focused.

7. **Reward proper planning and preparation.**
   Never do for the participants what they can do for themselves, whether that is getting materials for their table or having the tools they need for the next working session. Bring in a little competition by giving rewards to the group that has everything ready first. Another way to give rewards is by awarding points to all teams that are prepared for the next exercise within sixty seconds. This encourages the learning peers to help the unprepared students also get ready without anyone realizing what you are doing. It helps the unprepared without embarrassing them.

8. **Separate groups into complete and incomplete homework.**
   If learners have done the pre-work, honor that. Break the class into

two groups: those who have completed the homework and those who have not. Assure the learners that it doesn't matter which group they are in. You will have two activities ready. The unprepared's exercise will be the homework that should have been done in advance of the class. The other group will have an activity that builds on the knowledge they already have in regard to the content. This way, the second group is not revisiting everything they did before coming to class.

9. **Breathe.**

    Do not get exacerbated by the unprepared. It is their fault they did not do the work they were supposed to. Do not feel badly when they are unable to participate because they did not bring to class what they needed. Instead, take a deep breath, and continue to use the ideas in this chapter to encourage your unprepared learners. Know that you can always put an unprepared learner with a prepared learner and have them share tools to complete the work together. The group doesn't need to know that this wasn't the original plan. Don't apologize for what they may not notice.

10. **Provide an organization break.**

    Give the participants a list of "To Dos" and materials needed. Have the group take a moment to collect everything they will need. This is also a good time to have them do some housekeeping at their tables and clean up dirty dishes or scraps of paper that are no longer needed. For the organized person, this feels really good because they were living in a land of chaos, and the unprepared also feels good because they were given an opportunity to find items they had momentarily misplaced.

11. **Give prompt feedback.**

    This doesn't need to be an announcement in front of the whole group but needs to be done quickly to get the spontaneous off-the-cuff learner back on track. Work your way to the unprepared learner's table and quietly redirect this learner and help him get organized by asking, "What can I help you find?" or "It appears you might need my help; what can I do for you?" This is a gentle way to redirect and get him back on track. Consider using a non-verbal signal with him if this continues to be a problem.

12. **Share the why.**

    If the behavior continues, share with her why it is important to be efficient. When a class is efficient, there is safety. Help her understand it is not about authority, but knowledge, and you want her to walk away with as much as possible.

The Unqualified

Training touches every industry, company and individual role. Training drives productivity, safety, and quality. Training counts!

What happens when it becomes clear that an employee can't hack it in his job? Or when she's in over her head, truly unable to do what's required of her?

With proper benchmarks, learning objectives, and assessments, the training program is one of the first places the unqualified are discovered. They may have aced the job interview, but the skills and aptitude just aren't there. It's a sticky situation, and one you mustn't face alone. HR and management are your friends when it comes to managing performance. Here are some guiding thoughts to help you through that delicate dance.

1. **Design cooperative activities.**
   A cooperative activity is where learners work together to complete a task, help one another and grow as a group. An example of a competitive game would be something like basketball or any team sport. There's a clear winner and loser. In a cooperative game, there

are no losers because the focus is on everyone completing the task together. The learners are the decision makers, and the activity brings out leaders. The unqualified is able to ask a lot of questions and hear things explained in different ways. For instance, give every participant a balloon and have them blow them up and tie them off. Their goal as a group is to keep the balloons in the air while answering questions about the content or sharing what they have learned about the last learning segment. This is a revisit exercise that allows the unqualified to hear the content once again.

2. **Set clear expectations.**
Make sure you are very clear with instructions, including what the outcome of the project should look like and how it is to be done. Put these instructions in PowerPoint and allow learners to work on their own or with partners. Because the unqualified are drowning in the information, they are likely to be tense and unable to comprehend or recall the instructions. They will appreciate being able to look back up and know what they should be attempting to do.

3. **Do a human line up.**
Have everyone line up by how much they already know about the concepts about to be presented. This is self-proclaimed, and there is no wrong answer. If your unqualified person, let's call him Joe, puts himself in the middle, then pair Joe with someone slightly above him in experience. If Joe puts himself as the least knowledgeable of learners, put him with somebody in the middle. Do not pair him up with someone at the top of the knowledge chain of learners as this will frustrate them both.

4. **Promote partner work.**
The unqualified will likely lag behind fairly quickly. As soon as you see this happening, begin doing more partner work which will allow them to get the answers from someone else. In the process, they're still learning and still staying up with the rest of the class. A couple of ways to do this are:

- Use teachbacks. Have partners teach one another one of the concepts they have learned. Give them permission to give one another feedback if steps are missing or unclear. Now the partner becomes a coach. This helps the unqualified hear the right path or answer again while also helping their partners because speaking out loud increases retention and transfer of learning.
- Use pairs. Have partners work together to complete an assignment.
- Pairs and practice tests. If there is an ungraded practice test, allow them to work together and talk through the answers.

5. **Rotate table groups.**

    Because the unqualified doesn't bring much in the way of group discussions, brainstorms or completing work, they can become dead weight. By switching out tables, others can share the burden an unqualified person can become. If you see a particular group or person at a table getting frustrated with Joe, that's when you know it's time to switch table groups again. If you don't see that happening, then plan to switch the table groups twice a day.

6. **Use a variety of teaching methods.**

    Here are two different ways to have learners learning.

    - Gallery walk. Break the large group into smaller groups of up to five people. Provide each group with a different topic. Each group is then responsible for completing either a task or answering a prompt you provide on flip chart paper. Both of these provide an opportunity to discuss out loud while simultaneously being creative on their chart. After groups complete their charts in the time allotted, have them walk from one chart to another, learning from their peers' work. At each chart, it is the group's job to add one concept or idea to the poster.
    - Teachback. Participants prepare by reading a chapter or section of text and writing a couple of questions about the content on a 3x5 card with the answers on the back. To make it easier for the unqualified, do this in pairs. Then have them teach their small

group what they discover and learned from the text. The questions they create can be your revisit exercise later in the day.

For more ideas, read *CORE: Closers, Openers, Revisiters, and Energizers, volume 3*.

7. **Be patient.**
Sometimes the unqualified can be on the verge of a breakthrough if they just had another minute or two. Don't be so tied to an agenda when you see this happening. Allow for a bit of patience and flexibility with your schedule. Patience can also be displayed in answering yet another question or listening to them explain what they've learned in a painfully slow manner.

8. **Do regular knowledge checks.**
You want this participant to stay engaged, so it is important to do knowledge checks all throughout the session and not wait until the end of the day or course. This allows you to know how well she is doing or how far off she is from making it through the course. Regular quizzing will provide a better understanding of exactly which concepts she is understanding, if any. By being fastidious with your checks for understanding, you will be able to share with her manager specifically where she needs more work, if it comes to that. Having data helps everyone know where growth needs to occur.

9. **Use clicker technology.**
Clicker technology, such as TurningPoint or C3 Softworks, allows for a variety of polls and quizzes to be done. Creating a five-question quiz for each section of content allows for learners to privately answer and not be embarrassed when they get it wrong. The reporting in the back end of both TurningPoint and C3 Softworks allows you to see what questions were answered correctly or incorrectly by each participant as well as how long it took each person to answer the question. Turning Technologies' research shows that if it takes longer than twelve seconds to answer a question, it is likely the person is guessing. If you ask a question that requires higher order cognition or critical thinking to get

to the answer, disregard the amount of time it takes. Their brains need to work through the scenario to come up with the correct answer. The nice thing about clicker technology is that the results can be reviewed immediately.

10. **Provide succinct feedback privately during class.**

    As you see the unqualified participant's scores in your knowledge checks and clicker quizzes, give specific feedback during the class privately. Talk with him about the concerns you have and ask him what concerns he has about the course and the content. Make a plan together for you to continue to check-in throughout the remainder of the class.

11. **Offline conversation.**

    There may come a point where your unqualified participant is too overwhelmed, and it may be time for them to be done. Prior to this conversation, connect with his or her manager to find out what the manager would like for you to say during the conversation. Be direct with the manager and share the steps you have already taken and what you think should be done moving forward. This is a bigger conversation than providing feedback in the moment and should be done away from the rest of the class. This can be an emotional conversation for some and you want your participants to save face whenever possible. Follow the plan that you and the manager create.

12. **Document progress and share with the manager or HR.**

    If you and the manager decide an offline conversation is necessary, begin to document the unqualified participant's status previously and moving forward. Provide specific examples that include hard data.

Training Difficult People

The Vacationer

Any new parent knows the value of a good night's sleep. Josh was never a fan of attending conferences, but when he realized three nights away from home guaranteed three nights of uninterrupted sleep, he said, "Sign me up!"

It's not so much the vacationer wants to be HERE in training—it's just that here is better than THERE with a nasty boss looking over shoulders, potty training kids, and a dog that just ate a chocolate bar. "There" is back in freezing cold Narnia, a far cry from the warm, sunny conference venue, back in the daily grind with deadlines and demands.

Master trainers appreciate that not everyone in the room comes with the same intrinsic desire to learn. Sometimes here is just better than there. Or sometimes the intent is really just to kick back and relax. Next time you discover vacationers, try drawing them in with these tactics.

1. **Address the group.**
   If you are in a sunny destination and a majority of your participants are coming from the cold, plan to welcome the group by saying, "Good

morning to all my learners, and welcome to all my vacationers!" Wait for the classroom's laughter to die down and say, "In all seriousness, if I were in your shoes, it would definitely be difficult to not have my vacation hat on. However, while we are in class, I need for each of you to work hard and focus. Your reward as a group will be an additional fifteen minutes at lunch to give you enough time to take a dip in that beautiful pool, should you want to. If we work hard together, we might even get out a little early. I am making no promises, but I will do my best to make this training enjoyable and informational. Let's hear an 'amen,' 'yes,' 'woot, woot' or 'yeehaw!' if you like the sound of that." If said with the right tone and excitement, your class will be revved up and ready to go. You have just spoken the vacationer's language with a few extra minutes of vacation time at lunch and at the end of the day.

2. **Set learning goals early.**
Although you've gotten everyone on board, keep them there by revealing the agenda and what learning they have to look forward to. After they have a better idea of the content, have them write down two learning goals for themselves on post-it notes with one goal per post-it note. Have participants place the post-its on the flip chart you have made that says "Goals to Tackle" or something of the sort. If they have smartphones, they should take a picture of one another's goals so they can check-in to see where they are at throughout the session. As they meet their goals, they can take down the post-it from the chart or write "TACKLED" across it.

3. **Engagement survey.**
Make sure that your evaluations have questions that state "How actively did you participate?" and "How actively did your peers participate?" Allow the group to see an example of the evaluation so they know that they will be evaluating themselves on their engagement level as well as their peers. If you feel like your vacationers are on a mental vacation, include a clicker question that asks how engaged they are at this time. The choices could be: highly engaged, engaged, somewhat engaged,

somewhat not engaged, or not engaged. After you reveal the poll and see that some are not engaged, have the group do a physical energizer to get them moving.

4. **Create learning partners.**

    The vacationers need accountability. Do your best to split up the vacationers so they are with partners who are more focused. The partners can help take the vacationers from liabilities to learners. Whenever you see a vacationer arise, have her do an exercise with her learning partner.

5. **Use posters.**

    Because the vacationers' minds wander, have several posters up that reinforce what participants are supposed to be learning. This is all about letting vacationers go on a mental vacation but having them vacation in your world. As they glance around the room unfocused, they will see the flip charts and be reviewing content even if they're not tuned into what you happen to be saying at the time.

6. **Use competition.**

    Vacationers love to win free stuff. Apply that knowledge to the classroom and you will score big points with a vacationer. Create opportunities to compete against themselves as well as against others for random prizes. Pick out funny things like telling them they've just won a brand new convertible. Hand them a bag with a Hot Wheels convertible in it. To make it even funnier, have it be a used one from a thrift store! The group will erupt with laughter and the vacationer is thrilled, even if he was not the winner.

7. **Team leaders.**

    It is mid-afternoon, and the vacationers are getting restless. Have them be the team leaders a couple times in a row to keep them focused and on task. Make it appear random, and they will be none the wiser. Or ask the group, "Who are my vacationers?" Then say, "Thank you for volunteering to be the next team leader!" Again the room will erupt in laughter and you have your vacationers' attention.

8. **Provide roles to keep them on task.**

   These can be serious or funny. Try out some of the following:

   - During class, when the vacationer's attention is wandering, ask her to get you a glass of water.
   - Ask him to be a scribe and write on the flip chart.
   - Have her hand out materials or gauge the room's temperature.
   - Have him be a timer for his group's activity.

   It doesn't really matter what role you give them as long as it keeps them on task.

9. **Use practical application and practice time.**

   Practical application or practice time should be paired with an announcement that you will be randomly selecting three people to share their work or that, after they are done, they will exchange feedback with their partners. You have now notified them they are being held accountable. Provide less time than needed so they work hard. Near the end of time, feel free to announce that "it looks like we all could use a few additional minutes," and you can add time at that point. Use a visual timer so that the vacationer can see how little time he has left and stays focused.

BONUS: Tell the vacationers to go outside and check the temperature of the pool and discover the cocktail specials and report back. This tactic may result in quite a bit of dilly dallying, but it's a sure way to keep the vacationer out of your class for at least thirty minutes.

Where to Go

Below are articles and texts that I've read that either influenced some of my thinking on dealing with difficult learners or that can provide you with more information on each type of difficult learning personality.

Buzzkill
"Whining in Class" by Dr. Ken Shore, www.educationworld.com/a_curr/shore/shore009.shtml]

The Defeated
"Study strategies of college students: Are self-testing and scheduling related to achievement?" Hartwig, M.K. & Dunlosky, J. Psychon Bull Rev (2012) 19: 126. https://doi.org/10.3758/s13423-011-0181-y

Creative Training, a Train-the-Trainer Field Guide by Becky Pike Pluth. store.bobpikegroup.com/creative-training-a-train-the-trainer-field-guide

The Fighter
"Overcoming the Self-Promotion Dilemma: Interpersonal Attraction and Extra Help as a Consequence of Who Sings One's Praises" by Jeffrey Pfeffer, Christina Fong, Robert Cialdini, and Rebecca Portnoy. *Personality and Social Psychology Bulletin* 32(10):1362-74. November 2006. DOI: 10.1177/0146167206290337. https://www.researchgate.net/publication/6826554_Overcoming_the_Self-Promotion_Dilemma_Interpersonal_Attraction_and_Extra_Help_as_a_Consequence_of_Who_Sings_One%27s_Praises

The Hangry
"Low glucose relates to greater aggression in married couples." Brad J. Bushman, C. Nathan DeWall, Richard S. Pond, Jr., and Michael D. Hanus PNAS 2014 111 (17) 6254-6257; published ahead of print April 14, 2014, doi:10.1073/pnas.1400619111

The Petty Rule Breaker
"7 rules for rule breakers" by Alexandra Samuel: www.alexandrasamuel.com/world/7-rules-for-rule-breakers

"14 psychological forces that make good people do bad things" by Dr. Travis Bradberry: www.huffingtonpost.com/dr-travis-bradberry/14-psychological-forces-t_b_9752132.html

"Why so many of us lie, cheat, and steal" by Ronald E. Riggio, Ph.D. www.psychologytoday.com/blog/cutting-edge-leadership/201206/why-so-many-us-lie-cheat-and-steal?collection=1075959

The Slowpoke
The long URL for the readability utility is www.online-utility.org/english/readability_test_and_improve.jsp

The Texter
"73 Texting Statistics That Answer All Your Questions" by Kenneth Burke https://www.textrequest.com/blog/texting-statistics-answer-questions/

The Unprepared

"Tips for teaching unprepared students" by Jennifer Patterson Lorenzetti. www.facultyfocus.com/articles/effective-teaching-strategies/tips-teaching-unprepared-students

"A summary of Teaching Unprepared Students: Strategies for Promoting Success and Retention in Higher Education" by Kathleen F. Gabriel www.lavc.edu/stars/library/docs/Teaching-Unprepared-Students.aspx

The Unqualified

"How to manage a deadbeat employee" by Susan M. Heathfield. www.thebalance.com/how-to-manage-a-deadbeat-employee-1918712

Other Great Resources

Creative Training: a Train-the-Trainer Field Guide

Cut your design time in half, increase learner retention, and have more fun!

It's the trainer's trifecta, and it can be achieved through Instructor-Led, Participant-Centered (ILPC) creative training.

By using a repeatable process and training methods that complement how the brain learns, ILPC trainers spend less time designing training yet see increased motivation and content retention. Everybody, including the trainer, enjoys the learning process more because it is interactive.

In this book, Becky Pike Pluth explains why creative training works and walks the reader through a step-by-step process so you can implement these methods, experience improved training results, and reignite your passion for training.

Contributors also include industry leaders like Jennifer Hofmann, Neen James, and Sharon Bowman to make this a truly formidable resource for both face-to-face and virtual creative training.

101 Movie Clips that Teach and Train

Using short clips from movies can relay learning points more dramatically and quicker than any lecture.

Let this award-winning book jumpstart your creativity for lesson planning or training design by providing you with the perfect movie clip for over 100 topics including discrimination, leadership, team building, and sales.

Each clip comes with cueing times, plot summary and scene context, and cogent discussion questions. All topics are cross-referenced so you can easily find the perfect clip for your teaching or training needs.

CORE! series

The CORE! series of books is a compilation of activities that will help engage your learners while ensuring your content is remembered long after class is over.

These activities for Closing your session with impact, Opening your session with relevance, Revisiting content creatively, and Energizing your learners will make you a learning legend and improve training retention.

Books in this series include general CORE activities as well as a focus on technical training, webinar training and one-on-one training.

Books in this series:
CORE! Volume 3
CORE! for Technical Training, Volume 4
CORE! for Webinar Training, Volume 5
CORE! for One-on-One Training, Volume 6

Webinars with WoW Factor

Death by webinar is rapidly replacing death by PowerPoint! But it doesn't have to. Make webinars effective and engaging.

Teaching online is a different animal—requiring different skills and a different energy—that completely exposes any weaknesses in your material and preparation. In this book, Becky Pike Pluth shows trainers where to start when moving to an online platform and what pitfalls to avoid along with explaining some of the basic webinar tools trainers can use to make online training interactive. Becky includes 40 activities that will help even a novice webinar trainer create an online training that has impact and builds in long-term retention.

Creative Training Podcast

Want to continue your Creative Training education? Becky Pluth has a Creative Training podcast series with more than ninety short podcasts already archived! Each Friday, a new podcast is released. From scheduling fails to authenticity, games in the classroom to the deadly sins of team teaching, these short audio clips will continue to encourage you in your ILPC journey. You can listen to them for free at bit.ly/BPGpcdcast.

Training Tunes Royalty-Free Music, Volumes 1-5

This music collection contains 80 original tracks of royalty-free music specifically designed for the learning needs of participants. Fast-paced songs for breaks and games. Songs of 90-110 beats per minutes for introductions and exits. Slow songs to enhance discussion and reflection times.

All these titles and more great resources for training effectively are available from The Bob Pike Group at www.BobPikeGroup.com/shop-products or by calling (952) 829-2658 or (800) 383-9210.